MOSES

Moses

A Human Life

―◆―

AVIVAH GOTTLIEB ZORNBERG

Yale

UNIVERSITY

PRESS

New Haven and London

Frontispiece: *Study for Moses Saved from the Waters* (circa 1785), by Jean-Jacques Lagrenée (courtesy of The Athenaeum).

The material on pages 129–137 originally appeared, in slightly different form, in *Bewilderments: Reflections on the Book of Numbers* (New York: Schocken Books, 2015).

Excerpt from "Tübingen, January" by Paul Celan, translated by John Felstiner, in *Paul Celan: Poet, Survivor, Jew* by John Felstiner (Yale University Press, 1995). Reprinted with permission.

Yale University Press books may be purchased in quantity for educational, business, or promotional use. For information, please e-mail sales.press@yale.edu (U.S. office) or sales@yaleup.co.uk (U.K. office).

Set in Janson type by Integrated Publishing Solutions, Grand Rapids, Michigan. Printed in the United States of America.

ISBN 978-0-300-20962-4 (hardcover : alk. paper)

Library of Congress Control Number: 2016941501

A catalogue record for this book is available from the British Library.

This paper meets the requirements of ANSI/NISO Z39.48–1992 (Permanence of Paper).

10 9 8 7 6 5 4 3 2 1

He is on the track of Canaan all his life; it is incredible that he should see the land only when on the verge of death. The dying vision of it can only be intended to illustrate how incomplete a moment is human life, incomplete because a life like this could last forever and still be nothing but a moment. Moses fails to enter Canaan not because his life is too short but because it is a human life.

—Kafka, *Diaries*

———————

CONTENTS

ACKNOWLEDGMENTS

WRITING THIS book has been a return, with a difference, to a subject that has always fascinated me. In the context of the larger biblical narrative, Moses as both "man of God" and, simply, as "the man Moses" has been with me throughout my teaching and my writing life. The difference in approaching this project is the challenge of confronting the "biographical" dimension of the subject. A "life of Moses" is, in the usual sense, impossible. Moses looms too large in traditional Jewish thought, veering often toward the allegorical, the irreducibly Other. Writing a "human life" of this unknowable figure seemed to brush against the impossible.

I therefore owe a special debt of gratitude to Steven Zipperstein for inviting me to participate in the Yale University Press series of Jewish Lives and, more importantly, for persisting in his invitation in the face of my hesitations. His warm support of my unusual approach to biography made it possible for me to conceive of this book. Anita Shapira added her voice in encouraging me to write about Moses. As coeditors of the series and outstanding scholars, Steven and Anita honored me with their openness to my work.

I am grateful, too, to the many friends and students in Jerusalem and abroad who expressed interest and shared ideas as I was moving ahead with the writing. I want to single out Betsy Rosenberg for her deep readings of the chapters as they emerged—in fine exchange, she offered me her newborn poems; and my agent, Sharon Friedman, whose vivid intelligence mirrored my work back to me. I also want to acknowledge the patient and expert guidance of Ileene Smith and the editorial department at Yale University Press. In particular, I am grateful to Paul Betz for his careful copyediting. And, as always, I want to thank my good friends, Adele and Ron Tauber, for their warm hospitality during my lecture tours in the United States: they have given me a hub for my many flights across the American continent. In Jerusalem, the Matan Institute, the Israel Centre, and Beit Avi Chai have hosted my lectures; while the London School of Jewish Studies has graciously invited me, year after year, to address its students. These lectures and the connection they offered with varied audiences have stimulated my thinking on Moses the man.

Above all, I am grateful to my husband, Eric, for his daily presence in my life. Through his constant loving companionship (not to speak of his inspired cooking) he gives me time and space to absorb myself in learning, teaching, and writing. Eric and our children, Bracha, Yarden, and Avi, together with their partners, Paul, Yael, and Tali, and their children, Miriam, Aluma, Zohar, Shuvi, Yasmine, and Amir, form an abundant world; they each bring their vitality, wit, and beauty to bless my life.

Introduction

I ONCE took part in a bibliodrama workshop at a Jewish Theological Seminary rabbinical retreat. In the morning I taught Bible and rabbinics, and in the evening I joined my students for the workshop. We were asked to enter the role of a biblical character, and I chose to portray Moses in the scene where he beseeches God to allow him to cross over the river Jordan and enter the Holy Land. As I began to speak *as Moses*, I found myself weeping. I couldn't help wondering why the use of the first-person form had stirred such unsuspected depths of pain. Who was speaking? *I as Moses* turned out to be a volatile combination.

The pathos of Moses' plight had always been with me in my teaching, but never so profoundly . . . By switching to the first person, I had released a flood of grief.

In a sense, I was allowing myself—my *I*—to be read by the text. I was undergoing a harrowing transpersonal experience: exposing myself to the gaze or hearing of the text. Moses' words were interspersed with mine; in their otherness, they were also somehow mine.

In this study of Moses, my *I* is both absent and present. However chastely I avoid using the first person, an implicit *I* has chosen, for example, to shine a light on W. G. Sebald's Austerlitz, by way of illuminating the figure of Moses, who lived millennia before him (see chap. 1). I have allowed Austerlitz to speak for Moses.

This *I* seeks light where it can be found, even in the dark places of modern Jewish destiny. This *I* is affected by intimate affinities with aspects of Moses' experience. There is a seepage between author and subject that runs both ways. In writing about Moses, I bring myself to bear on my subject. But conversely, in bringing myself to bear, I am affected by the singular presence of my subject. Alchemically, a third presence is created in the space between myself and my subject.

The psychoanalyst Thomas Ogden has eloquently described the intimate experience of reading as a meeting of voices:

> A third subject is created in the experience of reading that is not reducible to either writer or reader. The creation of a third subject (that exists in tension with the writer and the reader as separate subjects) is the essence of the experience of reading.[1]

This third subject is *I-yet-not-I.* Even as we speak, or read, or write, we are spoken; by history, by our own unconscious life, by the one to whom we think we speak. The encounter with another inflects my own voice. The otherness of a text, or of my own *I-ness,* both disturbs and seduces me. Across a threshold of susceptibility, I am touched, I undergo something that comes from the outside but evokes a profound inwardness.

* * *

A biography of Moses is different from conventional biographies in that, perhaps uniquely, its source material is contained in one main text, the biblical text. But while reading this text remains a creative and even unpredictable endeavor, as I have suggested, the biographical challenge is immeasurably enriched by the existence of the "supplementary" material found in midrashic texts.

These texts, compiled mainly in Palestine from the third to the tenth centuries, are amplifications of the biblical narratives. Gaps are intuited, turbulences are palpated. Based on ancient reading traditions, midrash arises out of the discussions and disagreements of the House of Study; it often takes its origin in homiletical oral presentations to the community. It carries authentic, even inevitable resonances of the biblical words. I have tried to attend to these resonances, particularly in relation to what they evoke about Moses' inner world, about the ways he is touched by history, by God's call, and by his own quest.

The inner world of Moses emerges into higher relief in the final phase of his life. For it is in the last months of his life that he describes to his people, in the first person, their shared experience in the wilderness. At the heart of his apparently neutral account of experiences and divine communications already narrated, for the most part, in the third person, are moments of almost uncanny personal intensity—notably, Moses' account in Deuteronomy 3 of his entreaty to God to allow him to cross over to the Promised Land. Moses relates to the people a moment when God refused to listen to him. This story, like a cry of unassuaged anguish, stands out from the chronicles of conquest in which it is embedded.

In the first person, Moses testifies to an unbearable encounter with God's otherness. He transmits this testimony to his people; without his words, they—and we—would not know of it: "And I beseeched God at that time . . . and God would not listen to me: 'Enough! Never speak to Me again of this thing!'" (Deut. 3:23, 25, 26).[2]

Here, Moses' *I* emerges at its most vulnerable—and is si-

lenced. How do we read this? We too are wounded and silenced. This short narrative, this small disturbance in the
chronicle, bears a trace of Moses' essential being. In it is held
Moses' singularity, his truth. It stands out, conveying his unique
sensibility.

The midrashic sages offer an oblique reading that sensi-
tizes us to this moment of rupture; they hear its resonance at
other moments in Moses' final speeches. They hear Moses'
singular voice, his *I* narrating to his people a private moment
of their shared past.

In these midrashic passages, Moses expresses his sense of
abandonment *by them*.[3] He reproaches them for their failure to
bring him with them into the Holy Land. Their empathy, their
prayers might have moved God to relent. An entirely—even
shockingly—human Moses stands revealed here. Speaking in
his own voice, not to God but to his people, he grieves their
lack of attentiveness to him.

A new field of encounter opens between them, where the
Israelites are called on, as human beings, to respond to Moses'
human singularity. If they had had eyes, and ears, and a heart
for him, they might have tipped the balance of his fate.

What is striking about such midrashic narratives is the respect that they pay to Moses' "undignified" self-presentation.
Resentment, anger, complaint—these play a role in his final addresses to the people. Rather than speaking with the impersonal
authority of the messenger, he lets himself be heard speaking
from that threshold of susceptibility that precedes thoughtful-
ness. In the poignant voice of autobiography, he emerges, and
pierces us.

This voice, amplified in the midrash, communicates Moses'
aloneness, his unknownness. Paradoxically, Moses has always
been largely unknown to his people, and to us, his readers. But
the sense of his opaqueness, of his hidden life, is precisely what
gives him verisimilitude. An inscrutable subjectivity haunts the

book of Deuteronomy, which is, in the Talmudic expression, *his book*.⁴ The biblical portrait of this singular figure is, of necessity, incomplete. If only because of his periods of unrecorded encounter with God, the man Moses remains enigmatic, as though he holds a secret.

The Sages of the midrash add lights and shadows to his portrait but, in a sense, only deepen its mystery. He resists our full understanding and therefore seems real. The biographical desire—to know him fully—constantly brushes against its own impossibility.⁵

I have tried to attend to these midrashic readings of Moses' unique being. Largely, he remains in shadow, and from these shadows his reality emerges. In this "Life of Moses," I am compelled to complete the biblical act of creation: to trace Moses' birth into a world of genocide, his infancy with two mothers, his youth as an Egyptian prince, his calling by God into a life in which he is to speak for God to the Israelites and for the Israelites to God.

This messenger, it transpires, cannot speak; or at least this is his own self-description: "I am not a man of words. . . . I am heavy of mouth and heavy of tongue . . . of uncircumcised lips." Mouth, tongue, and lips become the partial objects, the organs that hold the place of his singularity. His first response to God's call is a dual one: "Here I am!" . . . "Who am I?" (Ex. 3:4, 11). His unique life is lived in excess of any specific identity. In some sense, at least at the outset, he is prelingual and thus poignantly susceptible to the impressions of a violent world.

In this early state, he lives in a kind of suspended animation. Bearer of a traumatic history, he comes to enact the unconscious history of his people. Here is another paradox: at his most singular, in his speechlessness, in his unknownness, Moses functions as a living metaphor for a people in exile from itself. Or perhaps, more accurately, we may say that he exists in a metonymic relation to the people who are, at first, both his and not his. He is associated with them and comes to represent them at certain junctures of their experience.

From the kabbalistic perspective, Moses' speechlessness is viewed as a case in point of a more general malaise; the *galut ha-dibbur*, the "exile of the word," which is the condition of *Mitzrayim*—Hebrew for Egypt—with its harmonics of *tzara* (constriction, trouble), *meitzar* (narrow straits), *tzirim* (birth contractions). On all levels, from the metaphysical to the brutally physical, the Israelites must be redeemed from a death grip that chokes their expressive life. *Yetziat Mitzrayim*—the *exodus* from Egypt—comes to mean an impossible but essential birth from anguish.

The gates of Egypt are opened, but this redemption comes only *b'chipazon* (Deut. 16:3)—in a kind of convulsive rush. Unable to comprehend their own history, they cannot truly hear God's message or speak their own redemption. The development of their subjectivity becomes the project of the wilderness years, of their process of *receiving* the Torah, which was given at Sinai. At the same time, Moses, part of them, and representing them, undergoes his own process of coming into language.

This revelatory process is figured in Moses' repeated movement from the top of the mountain to its base. Ascending to the summit of Sinai, he disappears from the view of the people. Descending to its base, he transmits the messages of the divine; he speaks what he has heard. Reluctantly at first, he parts from the ineffable conversation at the summit, and reenters the human world.

At a critical moment in the process, when the people have been seduced by a Golden Calf, God urges him: "Go on down— *Lech red!*" The Talmud elaborates: "Go on down from your greatness! I gave you greatness only *for the sake of Israel.* Now that Israel have sinned, what are you to Me?"[6]

Shockingly, God interrupts Moses' spiritual joy, his experience of a unique "greatness" in dialogue with God. He is who he is only *b'shvil yisrael*—"for the sake of Israel." He is the translator of God's message, chosen to convey God's words with his full self, in the full light of his face. He is to speak to and for his people. What does it mean to speak for one's people?

Moses' destiny, it emerges, is to speak in his own singular human voice. Achieving a healing relation between this voice and the divine words is the task of Sinai. The man who, according to the Zohar, has a voice but no speech (*kol* without *dibbur*), will, like the poet, reach out to his listeners, "using words to express a moan: ah-ah-ah."[7] Meaning comes at Sinai. But Torah is, at its heart, poetry. "And now, write for yourselves this song . . ." (Deut. 31:19).[8] The meanings of the Torah are many; its ultimate passion is direct:

> Forgive me this, forgive what I am saying,
> Whisper it, less than whisper, like someone praying.[9]

In the end, he writes Deuteronomy, his own book. In the first person, he speaks his own unique being to and for his people. Though his relations with them remain fraught to the end, they are by now *his* people. Representing the traumatic history of Israel, the Moses figure will more largely come to symbolize Israel's intellectual and spiritual energy. He becomes its soul-root; his name is given to the Messiah himself.

Moreover, this singular being—the singularly masculine "man Moses," who becomes the "man of God"—discovers in himself an essentially feminine dimension. At first, this dimension is obscure to himself: he speaks with some horror of a vocation that might claim his *maternal* devotion (Num. 11:11–12). But as he elaborates on the fantasy of pregnancy, giving birth and suckling a child, he brings to light, however unwillingly, an acknowledgment of the human existence of the feminine. This acknowledgment, too, has a redemptive force: it opens up a universally available feminine inflection of humanity.

Associated with this femininity is a will to communicate, an acceptance of the human body and human relationality. Beginning in the experience of muteness and solitude, Moses moves toward a difficult and singular encounter with the singularities of his people. This too is what is implied in the mission of speaking *for* his people.

To speak *for* a Moses whose mission is to speak for his people is to be drawn into a particular kind of thinking. In this study, I allow myself to be provoked by Moses—to be called, challenged. Once in this role, I cannot be unchanged. I am only grateful for this gift, which attaches me to what is beyond me.

1

◆｜◆｜◆

Identities

BORN INTO a world of genocide, he is nurtured in fear. When he is three months old, his mother places him in a well-caulked box and sets him in the Egyptian river. In this way, she both fulfills and defies the Egyptian decree: "Every male child you shall cast into the river" (Ex. 1:22).

This is the stark framework of Moses' early infancy. The story is complicated by the palpable tenderness of his mother's gaze ("She saw him that he was goodly . . ." [2:2]). She hides him as long as she can, she lovingly waterproofs the box, she "sets" him into it, and she "sets" it among the reeds at the river's edge. Another woman, Moses' sister, also keeps her gaze fixed on him after he is placed in the river: "to know what would be done to him" (2:4). Yet another woman, Pharaoh's daughter, sees him in his basket and is stirred to compassion. Under the

9

watchful gaze of three women, he passes through death, from one life to another life.

THE EXILE OF THE WORD

His sister's desire to *know* brings him through. But it is the stifling climate of *not-knowing* that characterizes the world into which Moses is born. The narrative of Exodus begins: "A new king arose over Egypt who *did not know* Joseph" (1:8). The politics of genocide begin here. In the amnesia of a new king, the gratitude owed to Joseph—who had saved Egypt from famine— is forgotten, and with it all ethical consciousness. Suddenly, without warning, the shadows of envy, hatred, and murder begin to gather.

Not knowing underlies all of Pharaoh's persecution policies. His arbitrary eclipse of recent history generates a historical crisis. Rashi considers two possibilities:

> Rav and Samuel disagreed. One said, This was literally a new king. The other said, His policy was changed. "He did not know" means, He made himself *as though he did not know.*[1]

Whether he was actually a new king or a transformed one, it is difficult to imagine that he would not *know* Joseph—that he would not remember him or at least his historical impact. So Samuel allows for the possibility of repression, the strategy of un-knowing what one knows. "He made himself as though he did not know." He actively refuses his own knowledge. Pharaoh's mind numbs itself so as not to know.

Here, a chord is struck that will swell to epic proportions. In midrashic literature, the climate of *Mitzrayim* (Egypt) is one of *not knowing, not seeing, not hearing, not speaking.* Conceived in mystical terms, *Mitzrayim* is the site of *meitzarim*, straits, in which possibilities of memory, communication and understanding are narrowed. Here, even breathing becomes congested;

the impact of slavery affects the life-rhythms of the sufferers (6:9). The Israelites are at first incapable of *hearing* the message of redemption, because of *kotzar ruach*—literally, shortness of breath (Ex. 6:9).

The new Israelite nation is represented at first by a high birth-rate but not a single voice. Mutely, the Israelites undergo the various torments that Pharaoh devises for them. When, finally, at the end of chapter 2, we first hear from them, inchoate cries of pain fill our ears. Four synonyms for *crying* are used, creating an effect of crazed, wordless suffering:

> The Israelites were *groaning* under the bondage and *cried out*.
> And their *screams* rose up to God. God heard their *moaning* (2:23–24).

As though no ordered understanding is possible, the sufferers know only the constricted reality of pain, which has the sinister power to "un-make" the world of meaning.[2] The language of the text records the traumatized sound-values of this world. Unexpectedly, these inchoate sounds are registered by God in four responsive verbs: "God heard . . . God remembered . . . God looked . . . God knew . . ." (2:24–25).

In this way, as though unable to remain impervious to human howls of pain, God enters the narrative. His name is repeated four times, with the hypnotic effect of a significant and yet uncanny process. Repetition tends to reduce an utterance to meaninglessness. This God who is so suddenly responsive has been unaccountably absent from Egypt until now. His sudden presence makes palpable His longstanding absence.

Rashi comments: "And God knew . . ."—"He paid attention to them and *no longer hid His eyes*." Rashi marks this juncture as a turning point in the narrative. Where before God had been insensible to the suffering of the Israelites, He now hears, remembers, sees, knows. A successful connection with the divine has been made—no small achievement in the straitened

Mitzrayim world. Life stirs within a mute and darkened existence. To cry out is to breach the fatality of such a world.

The term that is used in classic mystical texts to describe this constricted condition is *Galut ha-dibbur*—the Exile of the Word. Language itself suffers a kind of alienation; it loses its force and is lost to human access. At its extreme, even the rudimentary visceral language of moaning and wailing fails to break through. The first stirrings of protest are therefore highly significant. In mystical and Hassidic texts, such stirrings, the cry and the groan, constitute the first movements of the divine within the human. They intimate an imaginable possibility— of desire, of prayer, of language.[3]

In the exiled state, language is repressed. A Pharaoh who does not know Joseph has denied vital links with his own past history. A traumatic absence haunts his realm. His edicts blunt feeling and awareness, even the awareness of pain, even in his victims. Eventually, this Pharaoh will answer Moses in their first confrontation, "Who is God that I should listen to His voice? . . . I *do not know* God!" (5:2). Pharaoh's passion for ignorance —and for deafness—will develop over the course of the ten Plagues as, time and time again, Moses and Aaron's pleas fall on deaf ears: *And Pharaoh did not listen to them.*

The portrait of Pharaoh's imperviousness even to his own suffering, the compulsive "hardening" of his heart, becomes a refrain throughout the Plague chronicle. Apparently unable to grasp his own history, he enacts a kind of traumatic absence from his own experience.

More poignantly, the notion of the Exile of the Word intimates the unconscious pathology of the Israelites, who are its true victims. Time and again, Moses will protest against his messenger-role: "They will not believe me; they will not listen to me" (4:1). And indeed, as we have noticed, "they did not listen to Moses as a result of exasperation [lit., shortness of breath] and harsh labor" (6:9). And again, "How will Pharaoh listen to me, if they have not listened to me?" (6:12). An epidemic of deafness makes language futile. How should Moses speak in such a world?

One powerful midrashic reading imagines God as holding the displaced consciousness of an inert people. At the Burning Bush, God introduces Himself to Moses as One who sees His people's afflictions, who hears their cries and who "knows their pain" (3:7). Here, God comments on His own sharpened sensitivity in relation, specifically, to human pain. Here again, Rashi glosses: "I have paid attention to contemplate and know their pain: I have not hidden My eyes, nor shall I block My ears to their cry." God, at this juncture, is *no longer unconscious* of human suffering. He departs from a habitual apathy, from an exiled state. But another midrash goes further: "Dead flesh does not feel the scalpel, but I do know their pain, which they themselves do not feel."[4]

In this radical midrash, God constitutes Himself as the site of lost feeling. A traumatized people are compared to "dead flesh." When God "feels for them," He, on some level, represents that stirring to sensibility that will restore the dead to life. Divine empathy becomes the holding place for absent experience.

UNGRASPABLE HISTORIES

Freud opens his discussion of traumatic neurosis with the example of the survivor of a "shocking accident, for instance a train collision." Although he is apparently unharmed, the survivor eventually, after what Freud calls an "incubation period," develops grave symptoms. This phenomenon of *latency* characterizes the traumatic experience itself. The fact that the victim was, in a sense, not fully present during the accident becomes the eventual ground for its delayed experience. As Cathy Caruth puts it, "The space of unconsciousness is, paradoxically, precisely what preserves the event in its literality." The paradox that emerges is that "the impact of a history is conveyed, precisely, as what cannot be grasped in the event."[5]

Trauma does not refer to the damage to the nervous system but to "the effects produced on the organ of the mind."[6] Here, fright plays a role, and the sense of having missed the experience. Belatedness is inherent to traumatic experience— followed by repetitions of the event in the form of nightmare and fantasy, attempts to master what was never fully grasped in the first place.

In the light of Caruth's discussion, we can understand the Israelites' "apathy" in the face of their own suffering as a traumatic response to the catastrophe of genocide. The Exile of the Word, which affects all protagonists in the constricted *meitzarim* world, is conceived in mystical sources as part of a metaphysical condition. But in its lived experience, there is a sense precisely of *missed* experience, of an unfathomable possibility. Charles Dickens's Mrs. Gradgrind knows there is a pain somewhere in the room, "but I couldn't positively say that I have got it."[7] For the Israelites, God holds that pain in storage. To appropriate their own pain would allow them, in the full sense, to leave Egypt. Clearly that will not happen overnight; it will require a process for which the wilderness wandering will provide space and time.

"WHO AM I?"

Meanwhile, in the world of exile, Moses is to play the central role. He is to be the redeemer, the spokesman between God and the Israelites, God and Pharaoh. He will carry words across gulfs so that they are made good in the world. To this task God urgently summons him: "Moses! Moses!" And commands him, "You shall free (*ve-hotze*) my people Israel from Egypt" (3:4, 10). These first words of God to Moses evoke from the outset the issue of *hotze*, of *extracting, bringing out*. These words emerge "from out of the Burning Bush," from the thorny complexity of human pain.[8] This is the site from which God addresses Moses, simply asking to be *extracted*, in His involvement with His people, from the closed world that is *tzara*, the constriction in which one cannot move without further anguish.[9]

An eruption from out of silence, these words open a channel in the depths of Moses' being. "Here I am!" he responds, in the manner of Abraham before the Binding of Isaac. A shaft has penetrated him. But his next words are "*Who am I?*—that I should go to Pharaoh and extract the Israelites from Egypt?" (3:11). Moses' reaction to the divine call is ambivalent: he is ready to serve, but he doubts himself. Like other prophets after him, he expresses his sense of inadequacy to the role that God assigns him. But his question, "Who am I?" stands alone, starkly separate from the immediate context, just as he stands alone among prophets.

For Moses, this is the essential question, "*Mi Anochi?* Who am I?" This is his intimate response to God's claim on him, "I am the God of your father." In midrashic commentary, God speaks in a recognizable voice, so as not to shock the amateur prophet: He assumes his father's voice.[10] But in all questions having to do with Moses' parentage, an ambiguity inheres. Does Moses in fact know his biological father's voice? In the biblical text there is nothing to suggest that he has any contact with his birth family once he is adopted by the Egyptian princess. The ambiguous reference to the father's voice begs the question: Which father? How well does Moses know his birth father's voice? God's voice evokes Moses' sense of dual identity. Quite naturally, in this case, he responds out of his own duality: "*Who am I?*"—"How does my identity qualify me for this role?"

For Moses the issue of identity is fraught with ambiguity from the beginning. The opening scenes of his story yield two mothers, a narrative of birth, death, and rebirth. Although the princess, in retrieving him from the river, identifies him as "one of the Hebrew children," she clearly regards herself as "birthing" (*mosheh*) him from the waters that are death to Hebrew children. And when Miriam hires, in the princess's name, a "wet nurse from the Hebrews"—Moses' birth mother—the arrangement is clear: it is a commercial transaction in which the birth mother is paid for her services. She suckles her own child "for" the princess.

Returned to life from the Egyptian river, Moses is restored to his mother's breast. But this is an ambiguous return: the true mother is a hired proxy for another mother. When the child "grows" (2:10), at the appropriate moment of development, his birth mother brings him to Pharaoh's daughter—a movement inward, into an interior—"and he was to her a son." She is now to all intents and purposes his mother. She names him Moshe—in Egyptian, "son"—and explains the name: "for I drew him out from the water." The Hebrew puns on Egyptian and Hebrew meanings for the Moshe root: her motherhood is based on her gift of life to the child, whom she has extracted by the force of her compassion from the fatal river.

Moses' double identity is subtly, ironically etched in his complex birth story. Son to two mothers, what does he know in his Egyptian life of his previous life? Does he remember his Hebrew origins? If this is a story of salvation, its parameters are fraught with questions. This story of salvation holds repression at its heart. The conventional narrative movement of loss and retrieval, trouble and resolution, is interrupted; Moses' subjective experience remains largely obscure.

When he is restored to his birth mother, does the milk of her breast taste the same as it did before he was put in the river? During the palace period, does he remember—or, is he told of—his birth mother, her complicated milk? The text is silent on this, but the rupture with his birth family seems stark.

THE UNCANNY BOND OF BROTHERHOOD

However, when he does emerge from his Egyptian cocoon, the narrative startles us: "Moses grew and went forth *to his brothers*, and he saw their suffering" (2:11). This can be read simply to indicate that his purpose was to find out more about the slave people who, he is aware, are his birth nation. On this view, he is intentionally reconnecting with a past that still lives in his memory. This would be reinforced by another phrase in the same verse, where the slaves are again described as his birth nation: "He saw an Egyptian beating a Hebrew man, one of *his brothers*." Perhaps, after all, Moses has always known of his kinship with the Hebrew slaves; on this day, he sets himself, as their brother, to *see* their sufferings.

However, there are other possible narratives. Perhaps, as we originally assumed, the young prince does not know of his connection with these slaves. Perhaps it is the narrator who refers to the uncanny bond of brotherhood between prince and slaves. This would then be a moment of dramatic irony, since the narrator and the reader know more than the protagonist. Or, perhaps, fraternity is precisely what Moses *discovers*, when he emerges from a clear and untroubled Egyptian identity. Precisely when he witnesses human suffering, a new fraternal consciousness arises within him. Once he allows himself to *see*, he arrives obliquely at a knowledge of brotherhood. This is the meaning of *va-yigdal*—"*he grew*": this is his first crisis of maturation.

In a fit of empathy with the victim, he kills the Egyptian tormentor—almost as though in self-defense. The next day, when he again emerges—as part of this crisis of development—from the palace, there is no *seeing*. Instead, there is a *hineh*—the shock of an incomprehensible event: two Hebrews in violent combat. The aggressor taunts Moses with his own violence of yesterday. To this, Moses has no response other than to flee the vengeance of Pharaoh. The discovery of "wickedness," aggression, and malice, even among the victims, complicates his spontaneous act of identification. Here, the word "brothers" is no longer used. He apparently recognizes nothing of himself in this second scene.

On this reading, Moses' separation from his origins is quite complete. It is precisely his brothers' suffering that intimates a strange kinship. Beyond conscious awareness, a profound chord is struck. Something of this notion is suggested in midrashic reflections on Moses' first act in the world. The infant Moses hidden in the caulked box or basket in the reeds is first perceived by the princess as a *na'ar bocheh*—a "crying youth." His cries elicit her compassion and her identification of him as "one of the Hebrew children." But the expression *na'ar*, youth, jarringly evokes a much older child. It disrupts the classic scene of womanly compassion aroused by a baby's cries. The Talmud comments: "R. Yehuda said, His voice was like a young man's. R. Nehemia objected: But if you say so, you have given Moses a blemish!"[11] In itself, this interchange between sages is deeply expressive. R. Yehuda focuses on Moses' voice, which is mature beyond his years. In objecting, R. Nehemiah intimates that such precociousness would be a physical peculiarity, a form of disability.

But another midrash carries the idea of an over-developed organ even further.[12] The *na'ar* in the text evokes another *na'ar*: "For Israel is a youth and I love him" (Hosea 11:1). In the words of Hosea, God loves Israel as one loves a young man who is volatile, full of turbulent energy. By offering this verse as a proof-text, the midrash suggests that Moses is precociously identified with his people's pain, giving voice to a transpersonal anguish. Perhaps it is the princess who hears the baby's voice as expressive of a larger trauma?

Her perception of the infant is also deepened in another

Talmudic reading: "She opened [the box] and saw *him, the child*" (2:6). "She saw God's Presence with him."[13] Perhaps she sees some kind of aura surrounding the child, as indicated by the double object in the biblical verse. Like the baby's birth mother, she sees in the light of love. Her gaze is filled with desire for all that the baby may mean.

The child Moses weeps and expresses a pain larger than he knows. The gaze of the princess confirms his original mirroring in his birth mother's eyes. But at the same time, a rupture now begins. Handed back and forth between mothers, one claiming him, the other feeding him, his identity becomes a question rather than a given. "Who am I?" he protests when God would cast him in the redeemer role.

The same Talmudic discussion interrupts the apparently unbroken narrative in which a wet nurse is hired. Before he is assigned to the Hebrew wet nurse, there is a suppressed episode in which many Egyptian candidates are tried out. This would be a natural first step, since the royal household would have retained a staff for this purpose. "But he would not nurse! God said, The mouth that is destined to speak with My Presence should not nurse from an impure source!"

This infant is fastidious, his mouth already haunted by his future. The primal bond between infant and breast is troubled by thoughts beyond his grasp. His mother is restored to him only after she is thoroughly lost in a world of phantom breasts.

Is it surprising, then, that this infant will weep with a voice beyond his years—as though he knows what he cannot yet know? Or that this voice will be imagined as representing a "blemish"? Later, at the Burning Bush, he will try to express a kind of dis-ease in the mouth, an oral blockage: "I am not a man of words . . . heavy of mouth and heavy of tongue" (4:10). And still later: "I am of uncircumcised lips!" (6:12, 30). This is the only direct description Moses ever gives of his inner life. It may refer to an actual stammer; more importantly, it expresses an intimate experience of, precisely, *galut ha-dibbur*, the Exile of the Word. In his mouth, a metaphysical condition takes on immediate reality. What he has to say, he feels, will be stifled at birth: no one will hear, neither Pharaoh nor the Israelites.

CONGESTED INTENSITY

Marina Tsvetayeva quotes Pushkin on the ways in which words can fail: "There are two kinds of obscurity: one arises from a lack of feelings and thoughts, which have been replaced by words; the other from an abundance of feelings and thoughts, and the inadequacy of words to express them."[14]

From Moses' own idioms, we understand that he experiences an *excess* of "feelings and thoughts," a kind of congested intensity, as sealing his lips. We remember the benign narrative of how he comes to nurse at his own mother's breast; but also the shadow version in which the obscure pain of a larger world haunts his instinctual life even in infancy. His natural appetite must yield to a destiny of *speaking* to God. There is a rupture between the uses of the mouth; some basic trust in the world is put in question.

In the wilderness, he will cry out to God his strangest protest at the role that has been imposed on him:

> "Did I conceive all this people, did I bear them, that You should say to me, 'Carry them in your bosom as a wet nurse carries an infant,' to the land that You have promised on oath to their fathers?" (Num. 11:12).

Moses' troubled relation with the Israelites is figured in a rhetorical, a preposterous question: What is he—a mother who carried a pregnancy to birth, or at least a wet nurse—that he should be so burdened with the weight of this people? Satirically, he projects an image of himself with the body of a woman, or some hybrid figment of an *omen*—a male wet nurse—with breasts to feed a hungry infant. The surrealistic fantasy expresses his sense that he is miscast in the role of nurturer. He was once the infant whose mouth was in some way mismatched with the world.

His protest is both poignant and grotesque, as was his original self-description as "of uncircumcised lips." Together, the hybrid fantasy—lips, foreskin, the male body crossed with a fictional female body—constitutes a "raid on the inarticulate."[15]

For the irony is that Moses who cannot speak can articulate so powerfully a fragmented state of being. Desiring to be whole, he graphically describes a composite identity. Body parts are attached incongruously. Desire and recoil inhabit his imagery. An inexpressible yearning can find only imprecise representation. Language is in exile and can be viscerally imagined as such. This both disqualifies him and, paradoxically, qualifies him for the role that God has assigned him.

"FOR THE SAKE OF ISRAEL"

In the moment of the people's greatest failure, the sin of the Golden Calf, God abruptly tells Moses, at the summit of Mount Sinai, "Go on down, for your people have become corrupt" (Ex. 32:7). "Your people," God calls them, urging an identity. The Talmud glosses this rather fiercely: "I granted you greatness only *for the sake of Israel*. Now, Israel have sinned, what are you to me? Instantly, Moses' energy slackened, he had no strength to speak."[16]

The greatness assigned to Moses was always involved with language. It is only in his identity as speaker *for the sake of Israel* that he can speak at all. He belongs at the base of the mountain with his people, who constitute the ground of his being. Hearing this, a weakness overwhelms him. Just when God is inviting him to advocate "for the sake of Israel," he is dumbfounded. What God requires of him *for the sake of Israel* is, in every sense, beyond him.

Buber's articulation of the paradox of prophecy comes to mind: "It is laid upon the stammering to bring the voice of Heaven to Earth?"[17] Here is the *burden* of prophecy that lies so heavy on the stammering prophet.[18] His destiny is yoked with his people's in ways that he cannot at first fathom. Heaviness is everywhere, both inside his mouth and in his relation with a people who are "his" only by way of a mother who has receded into oblivion. He has been shot into a future that he cannot recognize as his own.

SUSPENDED ANIMATION

However, if he cannot speak, it is because there are too many voices, births, and languages claiming his ownership. Like all identities, his Egyptian identity comes to him from outside: from the name the princess gives him, which is the name he bears, despite other possible names that brush against him in the course of the narrative.[19] He is the one who has been "drawn out" of death and who is destined to draw others out.[20] But he is identified by the Midianite girls as an "Egyptian man" (2:19). *"Who am I?"* Haunted by a past beyond grasping and a future not fully his own, handed from mother to mother, he lives in a state of suspended animation. Even as his destiny is revealed to him, he has yet, in a sense, to be born.

One startling midrash traces God's promise at the Burning Bush—"I will be with your mouth and I will *teach* you (*ve-hore-iticha*) what to speak" (4:12)—to the root *harah*, "I will *conceive* you," "I will create you anew" (lit., "as a new creation").[21] Instead of curing Moses of his speech problem, God reaffirms the paradox that Buber articulates. Moses' mouth is precisely what God has chosen. But He will *be with his mouth*, He will implicate Himself in the issues of his mouth. God invites Moses to open his whole being to a kind of rebirth. Already twice-born, he is to surrender to yet another transfiguration. This midrashic reading is of course well submerged in the text, a repressed meaning that alludes to repressed meanings in Moses' life.

The need for an unrealized part of his being to come to light haunts his childhood and youth. On one level, this means a full awareness of his double identity, a deeper acknowledgment of the ways in which he is indeed of and for his Israelite people. On another level, frozen voices of pain within him ask to become audible.[22] It is precisely through his mouth that he will reclaim his own experience.

In the meantime, Moses is, in the words of the midrash, a "novice prophet."[23] In other words, a *na'ar*, still the precocious infant-youth crying in the reeds, still anticipating a destiny unrealized. He lives *within* closed spaces, hidden in his mother's house; in the box, in the river; in the palace; burying the dead Egyptian in the sand; hearing God calling from within the Bush, hiding his hand within his bosom. God urges him to "bring forth" what is incubating within him: to utter, to redeem, to expose to the light. The submerged is to emerge. The prospect is daunting, as when God stages for him his own hand emerging from his bosom, "leprous as snow" (4:6). Everything is at risk, to the limit of life itself.

LOST IDENTITIES: DERONDA AND AUSTERLITZ

This stage of suspended animation characterizes the experience of lost identity in European novels of the nineteenth and twentieth centuries. Indeed, in some works the theme of lost *Jewish* identity, as a personal and a national condition, quite pointedly invokes the Moses-foundling situation. These works deflect our reading of Moses' life so as to bring the question of his identity, shadows and all, from the margins into the center.

Take, for instance, two major novels, George Eliot's *Daniel Deronda* and W. G. Sebald's *Austerlitz*. In George Eliot's novel, the hero grows up as son of an English aristocrat. In his twenties, he discovers that his parents are European and Jewish. His mother reveals how, as an ambitious young singer, she gave him to a friend, an English aristocrat, to rear as his own. This common theme in Victorian literature—the abandoned child, the lost parents—is here complicated by the fact that Deronda acquires a more illustrious pedigree when he is thus adopted; and, at the same time, loses the hidden majesty of his Jewish ancestry.

Beyond the plot-dimension, George Eliot centers her novel on the state of suspended animation in which Deronda finds himself during the years before his origin is revealed. He suffers from an "oppressive skepticism, which represented his particular lot," from an "afflicting doubtfulness" about how much weight to give this pervasive emotional experience. His anger with his mother for robbing him of his "birthright" is set against her passionate rebellion against her father who imposed that birthright, with all its constraints, upon her.

The indecisiveness, the double darkness from which Deronda suffers is shot through with hope when he meets Mordecai, the impoverished Jewish intellectual who "adopts" him as his spiritual heir, at first without any evidence that he is, in fact, Jewish. The transitional state that Deronda inhabits before his mother reveals the truth gives its tone to the whole book, and particularly to Deronda's interest in Gwendolen's character and moral situation. This is a state of uncanny longing for some other world of identity and commitment. His energies are becalmed yet restless. He feels himself subject to what he later describes as an "inherited yearning—the effect of brooding thoughts in many ancestors."

> Suppose the stolen offspring of some mountain tribe brought up in a city of the plain, or one with an inherited genius for painting, and born blind—the ancestral life would lie within them as a dim longing for unknown objects and sensations, and the spell-bound habit of their inherited frames would be

like a cunningly-wrought musical instrument, never played
on, but quivering throughout in uneasy mysterious moanings
of its intricate structure that, under the right touch, gives
music. Something like that, I think, has been my experience.[24]

Moses is invoked to represent the unconscious preparation
for a great destiny offered by "another" identity and culture:

> And if it seems that the erring and unloving wills of men
> have helped to prepare you, as Moses was prepared, to serve
> your people better, that depends on another order than the
> law which must guide our footsteps (641).

Like Moses, Deronda has been guided by an ethical desire.
But dark intimations have haunted him, exacerbating the "dou-
bleness" in which he lives. Identified by others as Jewish, he
lacks the memories that might confirm such an identity. Un-
willing to disappoint Mordecai, or his own dreams, he is nevertheless reluctant to yield to wishful thinking.

Once his ancestry is established, Deronda assumes with
joy the obligation that both he and Mordecai envision: to lead
the Jewish people to their ancestral home in Palestine. Personal
identity and national salvation reflect and engender each other.
His mother's worst fears are fulfilled, as is his grandfather's
dearest desire. "Every Jew should rear his family as if he hoped
that a Deliverer might spring from it" (568).

If the figure of Moses haunts George Eliot's narrative of
redemption, it plays a different role in W. G. Sebald's meditation on bereavement and bereftness. Austerlitz is the foundling
raised to a life of unfathomable anxiety by a bleak Welsh couple
who adopt him as a Jewish *Kindertransport* refugee from Prague.
Exiled child of doomed parents, he is haunted by visions of star-
shaped fortresses, of fog and trains and windmills. His native
tongue dies away after lingering for a while, "like something
shut up and scratching or knocking, something which, out of
fear, stops its noise and falls silent whenever one tries to listen

to it" (138).[25] His Jewish childhood returns to him only after a breakdown and the accidental overhearing of a radio broadcast in which another survivor recounts her memories.

It returns, however, in spectral form, through the memories of his nanny in Prague, through hallucinatory fragments perceived as he travels by the same train route, from Prague to London, as in childhood; and through his fantasy of a twin brother, who had been with him during that long journey, "and whenever I thought of him I was tormented by the notion that toward the end of the journey he had died of consumption and was stowed in the baggage net with the rest of our belongings" (225).

Austerlitz knows only of loss—a cloudy apprehension that is gradually filled out by fantasy as much as by facts. He is the dead child whose losses become palpable. In the following passage, he remembers the Welsh children's Bible where he had learned by heart the chapter "about the confounding of the languages of the earth" (55). He remembers then

> how anxious I felt at the time when I read the tale of the daughter of Levi, who made an ark of bulrushes and daubed it with slime and with pitch, placed the child in the ark and laid it among the reeds by the side of the water—*yn yr hesg as fin yr afon*, I think that was how it ran. Further on in the story of Moses, said Austerlitz, I particularly liked the episode where the children of Israel cross a terrible wilderness, many days' journey long and wide, with nothing in sight but sky and sand as far as the eye can see. I tried to picture the pillar of cloud going before the people on their wanderings "to lead them the way," as the Bible puts it, and I immersed myself, forgetting all around me, in a full-page illustration showing the desert of Sinai looking just like the part of Wales where I grew up. . . . I knew that my proper place was among the tiny figures populating the camp. I examined every square inch of the illustration, which seemed to me uncannily famil-

iar. I thought I could make out a stone quarry in a rather
lighter patch on the steep slope of the mountain over to the
right, and I seemed to see a railway track in the regular curve
of the lines below it. But my mind dwelt chiefly on the fenced
square in the middle and the tent-like building at the far end,
with a cloud of white smoke above it. Whatever may have
been going on inside me at the time, the children of Israel's
camp in the wilderness was closer to me than life in Bala,
which I found more incomprehensible every day. (55–58)

Austerlitz is possessed by an alternative life, in a Welsh Sinai
wilderness, complete with a camp, a quarry, a railway track, a
tent-building (Holy of Holies!), which emits ambiguous smoke.
Biblical quotations return to him in Welsh, the language of his
amnesia. He includes the double-paged illustration from his
children's Bible, which he had examined so minutely. The sense
of something "uncannily familiar" finds nothing in reality to
ground it. Instead, it creates an uncanny longing.

Unlike Deronda, Austerlitz achieves no sense of salvation,
only rejection and annihilation. Anxiety attacks follow his discovery of identity, affecting his tongue and palate, "as dry as
if I had been lying in the desert for days." His heart palpitates
in his throat; he feels like screaming but cannot utter a sound
(228–29). These traumatic symptoms again pick up associations
with the history of Moses, dumbfounded, heavy of mouth and
heavy of tongue, encumbered by uncircumcised lips.

Born into a world of genocide, Austerlitz is a modern rein-
carnation of the biblical Moses figure, who, even in infancy,
wept in unconscious solidarity with his people's pain. Sebald in-
vests Austerlitz with just such a sensibility. Austerlitz is haunted
by his memory of a sixteenth-century Belgian painting, particularly of a woman fallen on the ice: "I feel as if [this] moment
. . . had never come to an end, as if the canary-yellow lady had
only just fallen over or swooned . . . as if the little accident . . .
were always happening over and over again, and nothing and

no one could ever remedy it" (13–14). With anguished accuracy, he speaks "at length about the marks of pain which, as he said he well knew, trace countless fine lines through history" (14).

Daniel Deronda and Austerlitz become reference points for a history, both personal and transpersonal, of identity lost and, in a sense, found. In Deronda's case, the kernel of Jewish identity is revealed, after yearning, intimations, and encounters that engender a coherent sense of historical purpose. The unplayed instrument is well and truly played. For Austerlitz, identity and purpose are known only as forever lost, poignant eruptions from unseen worlds. The self is dispersed, helpless, abandoned. At the heart of this melancholy world, Sebald writes elsewhere, is the "realization of the impossibility of salvation."[26]

MOSES AS EPIC PRECURSOR

For Moses, the question of the *possibility* of salvation is precisely what places him in a field in which Deronda and Austerlitz represent counterforces. Between the Deronda image of the redeemer, who will lead his people from exile to the Promised Land, and the inconsolable sorrow of history embodied in the figure of Austerlitz, the Moses figure is identified in kabbalistic literature as the soul-root of Israel. His history is the history of his people. All will receive the Torah through him; when he moves his lips to convey the sacred text, their lips move as well. In the Talmud, a brilliant reading of the text is celebrated with the words, "Moses, you have spoken well!"[27] In a sense, his life is both singular and metaphoric of the life of Israel. It will be consummated in the ultimate redemptive figure of the Messiah.

But his history, like theirs, only gradually emerges from exile and rupture. Latency and impediment mark his history. His birth into language plays out larger processes, divine processes of coming-to-be in the world. His identity, like Jewish identity and divine identity ("What is His Name?") will find oblique expression in the volatile world of *becoming* (*Ehyeh asher ehyeh*—"I shall become what I shall become"). Lostness will find itself in a language shaped by desire and fantasy. Woven throughout the tapestry of his life is the question of the *possibility* of redemption. In this sense, both Austerlitz and Deronda haunt our reading of Moses. They sharpen and deflect our perception of their epic precursor.[28]

ENGAGING A DEPTH WORLD

Is salvation then possible? In other words, do God's words, His promises, hold good? At the moment of greatest pressure, when His promises have, apparently, failed the test of history, Moses cries out: "O God! Why have You done evil to this people? Why then did you send me? Since I came to Pharaoh to speak in Your name, he has made things worse for Your people: *You have not saved Your people!*" (Ex. 5:22–23). Moses here brushes against the unspeakable. God's words have not merely been ineffective in bringing about salvation; they have proved *meaningless* in the ruthless press of reality, which is Pharaoh's realm. The *meitzarim*, the straits of senseless suffering, close in on the hopes of flesh and blood. This is the true "evil" of which Moses speaks: God's words ring hollow in human perception.

In this crisis, God responds: "*Now you shall see* what I will do." As if to intimate that the story proper begins only now, God speaks of this breaking point as a turning point. In the writings of R. Yaakov Leiner, the scion of the Ishbitz line of Hassidic masters, this critical moment becomes a paradigm of the salvation process. Moses' cry of outrage is to be the trigger of a redemption delayed till now. God's promises have awakened hope in the people, but till now they have remained unconsummated. A paradoxical process is necessary. God's words must go through a process of *exile*, of breaking apart, as in the original process of world creation, when an absolute Presence shattered into brilliant fragments.

The historical moment of deepest disappointment, like that original Breaking of the Vessels, reenacts the Exile of the Word in its metaphysical mode. What follows is a Redemption of the Word—"fulfilling His utterances, so that *they should not be lost;* then salvation will be fully consummated."[29]

What is gained through the process of loss and retrieval is the involvement of human work in the historical enactment of salvation. Even the human cry of outrage is human work. Such cries of pain are heard as forms of prayer, giving the sufferer an active role in the resolution of his suffering.

R. Leiner cites Proverbs: "Plans are foiled for want of counsel (*b'ein sod*), but they succeed through many advisors" (15:22). He translates: "When good thoughts occur and are *immediately lost,* this is because *ein sod,* because they do not emerge from the hidden depths of the heart." R. Leiner seizes on a singularly modern moment of awareness, the moment of "forgetting," of the loss of consciousness. In order to absorb the message of redemption, deep work is necessary, "from the depths of the heart." Without this, words, even divine words, are constantly in danger of being lost, of dissolving into exile.

To bring them to consummation, a surface coherence must be lost. A depth world, a fantasy world, is to be engaged: perhaps the paralyzing fantasy of the master-slave relation, of the irresistible *gezera,* the edict of the *Mitzrayim* realm, whose law is constriction. The power of these conditions lies in the fact that they are not only external, imposed by others: they live in the internal world of the victim, answering to unconscious fears and desires.

In this reading, things get worse before they get better. This is the pattern: suffering, hope, and worse suffering. Here, Pharaoh responds to God's demand, "Let My people go!" by tightening the vise still further (Ex. 5:1–10). In fact, the pattern is set from the beginning. Pharaoh's decree that midwives dispose of male Hebrew infants is foiled, only to be followed by a harsher, more official decree: *All* Egyptians are to be involved in the drowning of *all* Israelite male infants (1:22).

In this crisis, the Israelites face down their own terror and continue to bear children. The individual narrative of Moses' birth serves partially as a metaphor for the Israelite opening to life in a time of genocide. Here again, his story is both singular and representative. In midrashic diffractions of the episode, Moses' father at first separates from his wife in the terror of the times. His daughter Miriam compels him to see that he is in effect submitting to Pharaoh's decree. ("Your decree is worse than Pharaoh's," she says; "He decrees against male children, you against all children!" He is doing Pharaoh's work of constriction for him, only more effectively!) As a result, he returns to his wife and rescinds his own decree that all Israelite couples separate.[30] Babies are born: among them Moses—*primus inter pares.*

SPEAKING AND STAMMERING: PAUL CELAN

Only in this way will God's words hold good. The rupture, the experience of loss, of forgetting one's own thoughts, must be plumbed in order to reach to the depths of fantasy, of fear and desire, where thoughts come together or break apart. The breaking point, the site of trauma, is the site of human words, where losses may be, as Paul Celan puts it, *unlost.* This involves keeping terror and courage, the "No and Yes," the fullness of the void, un-split.[31]

Paul Celan is yet another modern victim of the Exile of the Word, estranged from what had been most familiar. He insists on writing in German, his mother language, which is also the language of those who murdered his mother, a language forever haunted by its demonic uses during the Holocaust. "As for me I am on the outside," he once said.[32] Ann Carson elaborates, "In order to write poetry at all, he had to develop an outside relationship with a language he had once been inside."[33]

This passage from his speech at Bremen has often been quoted:

> Reachable, near and unlost amid the losses, this one thing remained: language. This thing, language, remained unlost, yes, in spite of everything. But it had to go through its own loss of answers, had to go through terrifying muteness, had to go through the thousand darknesses of deathbringing talk.[34]

"Unlost amid the losses," sole survivor is language, even compromised language. It has to be "gone through" in its "answerlessness" (lit., "loss of answers"). In order to be *unlost, its lostness* has to be seen through, not resisted, not short-circuited, in all its terror. The "thousand darknesses of deathbringing talk" is a reference to the Nazi use of language as a means of genocide: "slogans, pseudo-scientific dogma, propaganda, euphemism."[35] Ann Carson suggests that for Celan language-death may have meant a more universal problem affecting the whole sphere of human communication: "the tendency of meanings to 'burn out' of language and to be covered over by a 'load of false and disfigured sincerity.'"[36]

This tendency of language as such is perhaps implicit in the midrashic readings of the Egyptian genocide. In one famous instance, when Pharaoh imposes slave labor *b'ferech*, "with harshness," the Sages read *b'feh rach*, "with soft language." Slogans, propaganda, euphemism—the political means of genocide. Or perhaps even a style of speaking that evokes a general ailment of communication—the tendency of meaning to burn out of language. Pharaoh becomes the paradigm of this tendency, as, for Celan, the thousand-year Reich brought the death of language to its nullest place.

What is left for Celan but to "go through" this death, this

answerlessness, this thorn bush, from which speech must emerge? For Moses, archetype of those for whom language no longer holds good, a similar passage lies ahead. If his people cannot *hear* him because of *kotzer ruach*—the pressure of impatience, exasperation, the desire to thwart the unbearable work of time, then Moses, crying out on their behalf, is already engaged in the work of "speaking and stammering."

> Came, if there
> came a man,
> came a man to the world, today, with
> the patriarchs'
> light-beard: he could,
> if he spoke of this
> time, he
> could
> only babble and babble,
> ever- ever-
> moremore.
>
> ("Pallaksch, Pallaksch")[37]

Something is being created through these stammering words, an area within which words may yet hold good. These are almost a private language—the babblings and repetitions that are all the prophet can utter. The German text ends in *zuzu* ("againagain"), which, Felstiner suggests, evokes the stammering prophet Moses: "I am heavy of mouth and tongue."

EXCESS AND INHIBITION

The tendency of meaning to burn out of language is a constant theme in Nietzsche's writings. Here lies the paradox of the stammer:

> May your virtue be too exalted for the familiarity of names:
> and if you must speak of her, then do not be ashamed to stam-

mer of her. Then speak and stammer, "This is *my* good; this I love; it pleases me wholly; thus alone do *I* want the good. I do not want it as divine law; I do not want it as human statute and need: it shall not be a signpost for me to overearths and paradises. It is an earthly virtue that I love: there is little prudence in it, and least of all the reason of all men. But this bird built its nest with me: therefore I love and caress it; now it dwells with me, sitting on its golden eggs." Thus you shall stammer and praise your virtue.[38]

To speak publicly of one's "virtue" is to vulgarize its precious idiosyncrasy. Nietzsche's solution is: "Speak and stammer." In a valuable essay, "Moses the Modest Law-Giver," Julie E. Cooper extends this notion to the issue of Moses' stammer.[39] Personal and inexpressible, his Revelation must not be travestied by easy utterance. The stammer, here, is part of the message; the hesitation, the halting delivery, the "fundamental inhibition of expression," convey the excess of revelation.[40] They may also convey the ambivalence of the prophet before the overwhelming influx of revelation. Fear and desire may create a dumbfounding conflict.[41]

The role of prophet or poet holds at its heart the paradox of speaking the unspeakable. While language is necessary for life within a stable social order, there is always "a loss involved as the multiple possible ways of experiencing the world are narrowed and channeled into what can be said."[42]

A certain kind of reticence, or circumspection, therefore halts the true prophet, faced with the inscrutable God, whose revelation must be narrowed into what can be said. In a moment of pure desire, Moses asks God, "Let me see please Your Glory" (33:18). God denies his request and grants him only a vision of His "back":

"You cannot see My face, for man may not see Me and live." And God said, "See, there is a place near Me. Stand on the rock and, as My Glory passes by, I will put you in a cleft in the rock, and shield you with My hand until I have passed by. Then I will remove My hand and you will see My back; but My face may not be seen" (33:20–23).

God's face cannot be seen by human eyes, but His "back," the traces of God's presence in the world, can be glimpsed *after* He has passed by. One of the Hassidic masters of the nineteenth century, R. Mordecai Yosef Leiner, known as Mei HaShiloach, reads the reference to God's "back" as a temporal reference to the *past*—to that which has passed and gone. Moses is given insight into past history, into processes already under way. But to see His face, or Presence, would mean to read God's meanings in the present moment: this is beyond human understanding.[43]

But this, precisely, is what Moses desires: to fathom God's ways in real time. So the Talmud describes his desire at this moment: "Moses said in God's presence, 'Master of the Universe, why do the righteous suffer, and the wicked prosper?'" This is the radical question, the core problem of souls. In a moment of divine favor, this is Moses' request, *Let me see Your face!* But God answers inscrutably: "The righteous who suffer are not perfectly righteous; and the wicked who prosper are not perfectly wicked!"[44] In spite of the unique intimacy between Moses and God ("He spoke with Him face to face, as a man speaks to his friend" [33:11]), a full revelation of divine meanings is withheld from him.

God is inscrutable on this most painful of human questions. Moses, in particular, is haunted by the unintelligible world into which he has been—twice—born. His life is, in some obscure way, a metaphor for that of the people to whom he is strangely attached. Why is he chosen? Why are they chosen, for genocide and for redemption?

Emmanuel Levinas, the French Jewish philosopher, remarks on the choice of Moses:

The language of the Old Testament is so suspicious of any rhetoric which never stammers that it has as its chief prophet a man "slow of speech and of tongue." In this disability we can see more than the simple admission of a limitation; it also acknowledges the nature of this kerygma, one which does not forget the weight of the world, the inertia of men, the dullness of their understanding.[45]

Moses is chosen because of his disability, which conveys not only his own limitations but also the human resistance to revelation. This resistance implies that the messenger will himself be afflicted by a sense of the clogged medium in which he has to speak. The language of the prophet will reflect this stalled experience; he will express himself through indirection.

Moreover, as Cooper argues, a kind of tragic realism requires the prophet to keep in mind the unredeemed nature of the world. An inherent silence will haunt the precipitations of speech. The most enlightened of human beings is nevertheless illumined only intermittently. This is Maimonides' image for the philosopher's experience of Revelation: like lightning flashes, truth appears and disappears.[46] A literary modesty must therefore mark his utterances.

Even Moses, for whom these flashes appear continuously, hides his face when God first speaks to him. Even he has imperfect access to God. Maimonides refers to the light that later irradiates Moses' face. It too is a subtly broken light: pulses, rays, rather than a direct energy. Both his reception and his transmission of the law have this intermittent though dense quality.[47] The truths that God would reveal are always indirect, with gaps and silences built in.

SILENCES

Silence, indeed, is an essential part of Moses' "modest" prophetic experience. A classic midrash interweaves language and silence, present and future time. Here, Moses envisions R. Akiva, who will expound the law with elaborate eloquence:

> Moses went and sat down behind eight rows [and listened to the future discussion of the law by R. Akiva]. Not being able to follow their arguments, he was ill at ease, but when they came to a certain subject and the disciples said to the master, "How do you know it?" and he replied, "It is a law given to Moses at Sinai," he was comforted. Then he turned round to God and said, "Master of the universe, You have such a man and you give the Torah through me!" God replied, *"Be silent! Such is My decree!"*
>
> Then Moses said, "Master of the universe, You have shown me his Torah, show me his reward!" "Turn around!" said God; Moses turned around and saw them weighing out his flesh at the market-stalls. "Master of the universe," Moses cried, "such Torah, and such a reward!" God replied, *"Be silent! Such is My decree!"*[48]

Throughout this midrash, Moses is bewildered: by the sophisticated discourses on the Torah that he witnesses in R. Akiva's academy; by R. Akiva's attributing them to him; by God's choice of him over R. Akiva; by R. Akiva's atrocious fate. Repeatedly, he turns to God with the words, "Master of the universe," asking for visions and explanations. And twice—on the two conundrums of God's choice of him and R. Akiva's gruesome "reward" —God answers him, *"Be silent! Thus is My decree!"*

On the two main mysteries that concern Moses—his own vocation and inexplicable human suffering—God is inscrutable. The mysteries remain opaque. Moses' bewilderment is, in a sense, divinely sanctioned. On such questions, words cannot hold good.

God's silence, then, makes possible both R. Akiva's flood of legal interpretations and his martyrdom. If God is inscrutable, too, both R. Akiva and Moses are given license: to speak and to be silent. Moses' role, though, is, as Cooper says, "ultimately more commensurate with the tragic dimension of life" under divine law. In his mouth, there is heaviness, opacity, bewilderment, hesitation, the quest for intimations.

Silence is justified, even required, where human life is more and other than we understand it to be. Nevertheless, God exerts pressure on Moses, in his prophetic role, to *speak*. When Moses resists, God is angry (Ex. 4:14). What would it mean for Moses, stammering, to *speak?*

Here is a midrashic narrative about the tension between Moses and God:

"These are the records of the Tabernacle": You find that when Israel were in harsh labor in Egypt, Pharaoh decreed (*gazar*) against them that they should not sleep at home nor have relations with their wives. Said R. Shimeon bar Chalafta, What did the daughters of Israel do? They would go down to draw water from the river, and God would prepare for them little fish in their buckets, and they would sell some of them, and cook some of them, and buy wine with the proceeds, and go to the field and feed their husbands, as it is said, "In all the labor of the field" (1:14).

And when they had eaten and drunk, the women would take the mirrors and look into them with their husbands, and she would say, "I am more comely than you"; and he would say, "I am more comely than you." As a result, they would accustom themselves to desire, and they became fruitful and multiplied, and God bestowed pregnancy on them [lit., He took note of them] immediately.

Some of our Sages said, "They bore two children at a time; others said, They bore six at a time; yet others said, They bore twelve at a time; and still others said, They bore six hundred thousand. . . . *And all these numbers from the mirrors* . . . In the merit of those mirrors which they showed their husbands to accustom them to desire, from the midst of the harsh labor, they raised up all the hosts, as it is said, "All the hosts of God went out of the land of Egypt" (12:41), and it is said, "God brought the children of Israel out of the land of Egypt in their hosts" (12:51).

When God told Moses to make the Tabernacle, the whole people stood up and offered whatever they had—silver, gold, copper, etc.; everyone eagerly offered their treasures. The women said, "What have we to offer as a gift for the Tabernacle?" So they brought the mirrors to Moses. When Moses saw those mirrors, he was furious with them. He said to the Israelites, "Take sticks and break their thighs! What do they need mirrors for?" Then God said to Moses, "Moses, these you despise! *These mirrors raised up all those hosts in Egypt!* Take them, and make of them a copper ewer with a copper stand for the priests to sanctify themselves—as it is said, "And he made the ewer of copper and its stand of copper, of the mirrors of those who created hosts . . ." (38:8).[49]

The mirror play of women in the Egyptian fields generates tension between God and Moses. Moses despises these mirrors, devices in the service of sexuality, vanity, narcissism. He violently ejects them from the sacred space of the Tabernacle. God reproaches Moses, "These mirrors raised up all the hosts of Israel!" He attributes the exploding birthrate among Israelite families (six at a time? twelve? six hundred thousand?) to the mirror play of women. At a time when Pharaoh's decree threatens the survival of the people, women stage this strange "boasting" scene: "I am more comely than you!" they claim to their mirrored partners, who are probably far from comely in their enslaved state. They provoke their husbands to vaunt their own beauty. And out of this strange game, a lost culture of desire and birth is retrieved.

More fantasy than reality, beauty is conjured by words spoken in a mirror. Mirrors reveal inaccessible visions: one's own

face, for instance, or the back or the side of one's head; tele-
scopic, microscopic, periscopic perspectives; laser reflections.
Words spoken in the mirror have the power to redeem the mortal misery of slave bodies. In defiance of Pharaoh's decree—
"Thus it shall be and not otherwise!"—babies are conceived, as
are anticipations, hopes for a larger life.

The dark side of the mirror, however, is that the mirror-
reflection is illusory. It is all done with mirrors . . . For better
and for worse, it is fantasy that engenders this redemption. In
the work of the French psychoanalyst Jacques Lacan, the child's
first glimpse of himself in a mirror, erect and coherent, provides an external prop for a fragmented identity. The infant
previously knew himself as "un corps morcelé," a body in bits
and pieces; now an illusory mirror image, a fiction of wholeness, will seduce him with an "ideal-I." The fragile ego continues to seek out such bits and pieces, fictions that offer the self a
stable identity, from the outside in:

> The ego is the sum of the identifications of the subject, with
> all that implies as to its radical contingency. If you allow me
> to give an image of it, the ego is like the superimposition of
> various coats borrowed from what I will call the bric-a-brac
> of its props department."[50]

This is an ongoing quest for identity. As Stephen Frosh puts it,
"The ego thus comes to be a home for lost desires and forsaken
objects."

For Lacan, this process is delusional. The self knows that it
is not really whole. Things fall apart; anxiety haunts the constant anticipation of self-mastery. There is a "constant danger
of sliding back again into the chaos from which he started."[51]
The tragic dimension of the process is inherent and inescapable.

In our midrash, however, although it is clear that the woman
is seducing her husband with provocative words about a fantasy
beauty, God defends the mirror game, fiction and all. For it

produces movement; there is a *lightness* to the intimate game; it *swings* a rigid reality of fragmentation (Pharaoh's decree, separating men and women) into a new "habit," a new culture, of desire.[52] In a world of *gezera*, in which things are forever as they must be, these women have modeled redemption. Those mirrors, fictional representations, not simply of an illusory self, but also of anticipated relationship, create openings to alternative worlds.

MOSES AGAINST MIRRORS

Moses' violent response to the donation of these mirrors to the Tabernacle is not hard to understand. This erotic culture is false; its language is seductive and builds on fantasy. Moreover, the issue of truth and falsehood has a personal significance to Moses. If, as we have suggested, his own sense of identity remains a fraught question throughout the early part of his life, the play with illusion and the blurring of boundaries—mirrors in the Tabernacle—would personally offend him. An ascetic aspiration for a world of truth would leave Eros a highly circumscribed role in human life.

"Who am I?" (Ex. 3:12) he demanded at the Burning Bush, resisting the redemptive role that God would impose on him. And again, "If they ask me, What is His name, what shall I tell them?" (3:13). Not a man of words, he nevertheless craves names, the language that pins down a spinning reality. God answers evasively: "*I will be* with you!" And gives him a sign to authenticate his mission: "*I will be what I will be! I will be* has sent me to you!" (3:14).

In this first encounter with God, Moses stages his own anxiety about names, about true words that will hold good. But God's identity is elusive; it holds transformation at its heart—a matter of *becoming* rather than *being*.[53] And so, apparently, is Moses' identity. Rather than pacifying Moses' imagination, God provokes it: "*I will be* with your mouth!" (4:12). God remains inscrutable, and His answers do not allay Moses' anxiety. Moses responds with silence.

So God then proceeds further to identify Himself: "Thus you shall say to the children of Israel, God, the God of your fathers, God of Abraham, God of Isaac, and God of Jacob, has sent me to you: that is *My name for ever,* and that is my *appellation throughout the generations*" (3:15). Finally, a name, an eternal name. But it was the Nameless God who spoke first, addressing the uncertainties of Moses' deepest sense of himself. The eternal name is intended for the people; but the Nameless God had identified Himself to Moses alone. *Ehyeh—I will be* evokes a Becoming beyond words: perhaps, indeed, a kind of divine stammer, intimating an inviolable privacy.

Moses' response passionately disputes God's open future tense: "But they will not believe me, they will not listen to me!" (4:1) And further, "Please O God, I have never been a man of words, neither yesterday nor the day before, nor now that You have spoken to Your servant. For I am heavy of mouth and heavy of tongue" (4:10). To which God replies by inflecting His nameless *Ehyeh:* "I am God [the Tetragrammaton, YH-VH—"*He who will be*"] . . . I *will be* with your mouth" (4:11–12).

If God is a verb, rather than a noun, then His support of the women and their mirrors becomes intelligible. As the God of becoming, He sponsors the infinite play of possibility: the hosts of Israel waiting in the wings. And Moses positions himself, strangely, in the opposition, aligned—still more strangely—with Pharaoh and his decrees. In the flux of identities and identifications, Moses seeks stability, a clear social-symbolic order. The women playing with what-may-be, with the fictions of possibility, threaten a proper sense of order. But what God implies is that the ordered is often the defensive: it is Pharaoh's constricted invention, a *meitzar*-device, narrowing what can be understood by human life.

In the midrash, these copper mirrors are to be taken in, incorporated into the Tabernacle, in the form of the copper stand and ewer used by the priests to sanctify themselves. At divine command, erotic and sacred realities are merged. Indeed, as Ramban points out, unlike other copper contributions to the Tabernacle, the women's mirrors were not melted down to be re-formed into the sacred accoutrements. They retained their integrity as mirrors, with the disturbing associations that Moses finds so offensive.

Moses both desires and fears language: he longs for the power of names to stabilize and unify experience, while he fears its dynamic, endlessly protean character. Fictions give birth to further fictions, till the ground of truth has been lost. Or, paradoxically, we might say that the opposite is true: what he fears is the limiting, narrowing effect of language, while he longs for its capacity to break out of the armor of rigid meanings. This second ambivalence is represented by God in the midrash, urging Moses to broaden his vision of the mirror reality. He is to find a way out of exile, specifically, out of the Exile of the Word that is the most radical manifestation of all exiles.

STORIES OF UNCLAIMED EXPERIENCE

In an unredeemed world, how can redemption be achieved? We remember Austerlitz's description of the sixteenth-century Belgian painting; the woman who has fallen on the ice comes to represent a fatality, the way "marks of pain trace countless fine lines through history. This is always happening over and over again. Nothing and no-one could remedy it" (14). In Austerlitz's mind, the sheer repetition of historical anguish, like a stammer, speaks of an irremediable state.

And yet, the painter's work, Austerlitz's broken narrative, and Sebald's complex framing of that narrative are mirrors-within-mirrors, performing a barely glimpsed possibility.

A certain kind of language may open the long-closed mouth. Even if all that emerges is the long-drawn out A-A-A-A of a Novelli tortured to the point where words abandon him.

Novelli's story emerges from Austerlitz's storehouse of memories when he thinks of the tortures inflicted on prisoners in the Breedonk fortress; he remembers Claude Simon's "storehouse of memories," among them "the fragmentary tale of a certain Gastone Novelli," who, after being tortured at Dachau, found the sight of a German, or of any civilized being, so intolerable that he went off to the South American jungle, where he completed a dictionary of the language of the tribe of pygmies among whom he lived. This language consisted almost entirely of vowels, particularly the sound A in countless variations. Later, Novelli returned to his native land and began to paint pictures, mostly featuring the letter A, formations "rising and falling in waves like a long-drawn-out scream.

> AAAAAAAAAAAAAAAAAAAAAAAAAAAAAAAAAAAAAAAAAA
> AAAAAAAAAAAAAAAAAAAAAAAAAA"[54]

Austerlitz connects his visit to the fortress with his later reading of the particular torture that Jean Améry suffered there. Another book comes to mind, a particular story. Silence haunts these unbearable memories, but fragments break through. Till Novelli gives his own fragmentary account, first in his scientific account of the pygmy language, and then in his paintings, which are pure representations of pain, an endless stammer.

Austerlitz, who himself stammers on occasion, and who at crucial moments cannot bring out the words he should have spoken, nevertheless, in a sense, redeems, by his linked associations, his unlived life.[55] At least, the narrator, or Sebald himself, in writing and framing the story, records both the impossibility and the possibility of redemption.

The Torah tells of a traumatized national silence that erupts into cries of pain—four different synonyms for the cry. Here language begins. What redemption lies here? Is the cry not simply the trace of pure pain, which "un-makes the world"?[56] And yet, as we have noticed, R. Yaakov Leiner would have us hear this cry as the "beginning of redemption": "Now, you will see what I will do," God tells Moses. At the darkest hour, when language, even divine words of promise, fails altogether, at that breaking point, what is lost may become unlost. The sufferer may open herself to an intimation, something emerging from depths never before fathomed. This is the work of the mirrors, which performs redemption in a different language.

Another Hassidic reading speaks of a people who can barely experience their own history. When God arrives at His ultimate promise of redemption, which is to demonstrate that His words do indeed hold good, He uses four synonyms: "I will take you out, I will save you, I will redeem you, I will take you to Me as a people" (Ex. 6:6–7). This is known as "the four languages of redemption": four repetitions that are not repetitions —divine stammers . . . But the Israelites, we are told, "did not hear" these words (6:9). Moses tries to convey this message of redemption, but the message falls on deaf ears.

Since the message took no root in their consciousness, writes Sefat Emet, *we* must keep telling the story.[57] More than that, since God knew what would happen, His message was intended to provoke precisely this sequence of repression, deafness, unawareness, followed by later retrievals. The effect of repression is the fertility of re-membering, of the effort to create coherent narratives in an experience of rupture.

The traumatic gap in communication is indicated, writes Sefat Emet, by the word *chipazon*, "panic haste." This expresses the inherent nature of such traumatic departures: "You shall eat it [the Paschal lamb] in *chipazon*" (12:11), God instructs Moses just before the Exodus. And forty years later, in retrospect, Moses remembers, "You left Egypt in *chipazon*" (Deut. 16:3).

The unassimilated experience of the Exodus is made good

by generations of storytelling. Each in its own language, the generations play out the multiple possibilities—the four languages—of redemption. In telling these stories of unclaimed experience, we fulfill a *mitzvah*, a positive commandment. From the unregistered power of the Exodus, Torah is made for all generations.

The implications of this passage are quite astonishing. Writing at the end of the nineteenth century, Sefat Emet departs from positivist readings of the Exodus: in place of the conventional narrative—"This is what God promised; the people heard and believed; God's words are fulfilled in an immediate authentication of the divine role in history"—he offers a world in which forgetting, unawareness, and silence are the breeding ground of fertile re-memberings. The languages of the descendants constitute a Torah-revelation that redeems the repressed historical moment.

"STORED THERE IN YOUR EYES"

How does this affect Moses and the history of his mouth? His mission is, we might say, to speak words, to Pharaoh and to the Israelites, that will not immediately come true. In addition, if we follow the clue of Sefat Emet's teachings, a built-in traumatic response will prevent the Israelites from fully registering both promise and redemption.

The main fact of their history becomes the repression of the event, as it happens in real time. Redemption and revelation happen both too late and too soon. On the night of the Exodus, they wait, girded and booted, for the moment of departure. Then it is upon them and they rush out of Egypt! There is something ungainly, both bashful and precipitate, about this redemption. A time lag is built in.

"The problem was that you didn't always know what you were seeing until later, maybe years later, that a lot of it never made it in at all, it just stayed stored there in your eyes."[58] History is no longer straightforwardly referential. As Cathy Caruth argues, it is in the encounter with trauma that we can begin to recognize the possibility of a history of a different kind. This may open the possibility of "permitting history to arise where *immediate understanding* may not."[59]

It is only in and through its inherent forgetting that the Exodus is first experienced at all. The story of Exodus, of a traumatic departure, will be revisited time and again in the Wilderness. Thus begins the ongoing history of *torah she-ba'al peh*, the Oral Torah—literally, "the Torah of the mouth." The narrator comes, at certain moments, to "understand in chords," sounding simultaneously meanings from multiple worlds.[60]

In this process of suffering, repression, and retrieval, Moses plays a key role. On the one hand, he is the singular repository of memory. In him is stored a fuller awareness of the meanings of his experience. He will remind the people, rebuke them, pray for them in their many departures from their own experience. In this way, he will represent the continuity of history.

But, on the other hand, as we have seen, he too suffers from the Exile of the Word, a speech-spasm like a foreign body in his mouth. His own personal history is fragmented, his identity complicated. Like our modern survivors of such alienations, Deronda and Austerlitz and Celan, he represents the very discontinuities that haunt his people. This too is his destiny; this too is a key to possible redemption.

2

The Murmuring Deep

JUST AS Moses has fulfilled the first stage of his mission—
to carry God's word to Pharaoh—his relations with God reach
breaking point:

> Then Moses turned to God and said, "O God, why did You
> do evil to this people? Why then did You send me? Ever
> since I came to Pharaoh to speak in Your name, he has made
> things worse for this people; You have definitely not saved
> Your people!" (Ex. 5:22–23)

Moses' words are suffused with anger, reproach, frustration.
As God's messenger of redemption—"Let My people go!"—he
has been miserably ineffective: Pharaoh's "evil," so far from
abating, has gathered cruel force; Moses has failed his people.
Ultimately, God Himself is responsible for the "evil" in which
the people are embroiled.

"Lamah—Why?" he asks twice. For the first time in the biblical narrative, a human being addresses God with the rhetorical *lamah*. Moses breaks new ground, uttering a new and provocative form of question, as though he has the right to understand God's dealings with the world. Using the word *Ra—evil* of God, Moses juxtaposes God's dealings with those of the evil Pharaoh. The Israelites are enveloped in a medium of instability, where God makes promises and then apparently reneges on them: *"Save?—You have not saved Your people!"* Moses cries with some irony, implicitly quoting God's promise back to Him: "I have come down to save them" (Ex. 3:8).

"Lamah—Why?" The demand for explanations has previously appeared only in human dialogues, in protests against tyranny. A few verses before this breaking point, the Israelites cried out in outrage to Pharaoh: *"Why* should you act in this manner to your servants?" (5:15). Now, Moses unconsciously picks up this *lamah* of protest and turns it against God, challenging Him in a new voice.

This voice of Moses represents areas of human experience never before plumbed.[1] Speaking in the name of human suffering, he protests against God's inscrutability. But since his relation to the people is ambivalent, he refers to them in two ways: as *"this* people," suggesting a relation of estrangement; but also as *"Your* people," advocating for them as objects of God's love. It is only at a later stage that he will speak in the voice of conscious solidarity.

In the midrashic traditions, God responds to Moses' reproach with equal ambiguity.[2] One divine impulse is to punish Moses for overstepping a boundary. But God transcends His own anger and acknowledges the authentic passion of Moses' new voice:

> R. Akiva said that Moses argued thus: "I know that You will one day save them, but what about those who will have been

immured in the buildings?" Then the Attribute of Justice sought to strike Moses, but after God saw that Moses argued thus only for the sake of Israel, He did not allow the Attribute of Justice to strike him.[3]

R. Akiva softens Moses' provocative cry: "Save? You have *not* saved Your people!" Moses does not mean to cast doubt on God's promises.[4] His reproach is more subtle: even if God eventually fulfills His promise, it will be too late for those who have been killed in the meantime. The gap between words and reality is one that human beings cannot easily bear. From the human perspective, the passage of time means many deaths. In the words of the midrash, "What do You care about those who will have been immured . . . ?" With every day that passes, more human lives are snuffed out.[5]

"What do You care?" This is R. Akiva's translation of Moses' "*Why* have You done evil to your people?" He is demonstrating the difference between divine time and human time. Does God experience the urgency of human vulnerability? This "Why?" is saturated with the pathos of mortality. "We—as opposed to You—have *no time* for delay!"

Divine time transcends the fragile condition of human life. For the first time, a human being cries out this radical *Why?* in the name of all that is not divine in the lives of his brothers. Instead of "speaking in God's name" (5:23), he speaks in the name of the dying.

The midrash ends with a complex divine response. The "judgmental" God (the Attribute of Justice) is poised to strike Moses down for his irreverence. But the compassionate God relents—when He sees that Moses speaks "for the sake of Israel." The Hebrew expression is *bishvil Yisrael*: Moses speaks for the benefit of Israel, for their good. But, as well, he speaks "on their behalf," in their name, representing those who cannot speak for themselves—the voices that are in constant danger of suffocation.

Here, God understands Moses in a newly complex way—as though He hears him "in chords," with meanings from many different worlds. What is it to speak, both in God's name and in the name of vulnerable flesh and blood? A double-voiced singer, like those Mongolian singers who can utter more than one pitch at the same time, Moses begins to develop the singular polyphonic ability of his double mission.

Here, he represents those who cannot speak for themselves. Among the four evocations of pain—groans, cries, wails, screams —which are the first sounds we hear from the silent people (2:24), is the word *na'aka:* "When God heard their *na'aka*, He remembered His covenant." What is a *na'aka?* In Ramban's reading, this refers to the death rattle of those who are immured in the Egyptian building projects. Ramban cites a proof-text from Ezekiel: "They cried out with the *na'aka* of those who are being slain" (30:24).

In Ezekiel's vision of the Dry Bones, the dead cry out, "Our bones are dried up, we are cut off" (Ezek. 37:11). Ramban quotes this: "We live like the dead who say, 'Our bones are dried up, we are cut off.'"[6] Ramban uses Ezekiel's macabre imagery of the dying, who cry out their strangled despair, in order to give voice to the fate of Jews in exile in his own time. This is a life-in-death, a speaking muteness, which only God can hear.

When Moses speaks *on behalf* of Israel, then, he acts as a proxy voice, amplifying and supplementing their inchoate sounds. In this role, he is forgiven for his irreverent tone. He is recognized for a new genre of expressiveness; he lends his vitality to the people's inertia. He is not of them, nor is he like them. He is separate from them—reared in a different world— and yet, he is in some uncanny relation with them that allows him to give voice to their despair.

God strikingly responds, "I too have heard the *na'aka* of the Israelites" (Ex. 6:5). As though to say: "You are not the only one to care about their fragility!" Once Moses has given voice to their strangled cries, God declares Himself his ally in empathy.

But if Moses advocates for a people who cannot afford to wait for redemption, he also speaks for a God who requires a human voice to represent Him. Strangely, it is Moses, with his "uncircumcised lips," who is the necessary mediator between the divine and the human. What does he, uniquely, bring to the "impossible" process of redemption?

WORDS AND VOICE

A remarkable suggestion appears in the nineteenth-century commentary *Ha'amek Davar*. At the Burning Bush, God charges Moses with his first message to the Israelite elders. He then reassures Moses, even before he has expressed any reservations, "They will listen to your voice!" (3:18). Moses listens silently to the rest of God's speech and then bursts out in protest, "But they will not believe me, *they will not listen to my voice!*" (4:1).

On the face of it, Moses cannot accept God's reassurances. So convinced is he that his voice will have no effect on his people that he directly contradicts God's promise. He feels mysteriously handicapped, incapable of convincing the Israelites that he, of all people, has received a divine revelation. He is, after all, only tangentially identified as one of them; he is not a plausible candidate for the leadership of a people with whom he has merely biological kinship. His sense of being "heavy of mouth and heavy of tongue" is perhaps the effect of his weak links with the community. He feels handicapped because they will not "listen to his voice."

However, *Ha'amek Davar* has a different reading. God's reassurance ("They will listen to your voice") is not simply a promise; it is a condition, a demand: "Only if you speak *with your own voice* will they listen and join you in challenging Pharaoh." In this reading, the whole scenario of redemption depends on this one condition: Moses' voice must be heard. In the event, Moses refuses to speak and Aaron is delegated to convey God's words. So the elders hear God's words, but in the wrong voice.

The result is that the scenario of redemption falters. The elders are not inspired to accompany Moses to the palace. Instead, Moses and Aaron go alone; they speak in the name of God ("Thus says God, the God of Israel, Let My people go, so they may feast for Me in the wilderness" [5:1]), rather than in the name of the people, expressing the will of the people ("The God of the Hebrews appeared to *us*—so now let us go a journey of three days into the wilderness" [3:18]).

What should have been a popular movement of spiritual enthusiasm is attenuated into the stark command of God. In *Ha'amek Davar,* the whole narrative is read with an eye for the discrepancies between God's scenario and what actually transpires—and the commentary concludes that since Moses withheld his *voice,* the redemptive process was, in important ways, disrupted.

In this remarkable reading, words and voice are differentiated. Moses refuses to lend his voice to the occasion. It is precisely his voice that he distrusts. But this voice is what God asks for. In his own voice, Moses might have affected and transformed their fate. In the expression of the midrash, "The Shechina (God's Presence) spoke out of his throat." Ventriloquist for God, Moses' voice might have inspired the people more poignantly than could the divine words alone.

Here, the whole process of redemption pivots on Moses' absent voice. But, we might ask, if his voice carries divine undertones, why is he so embarrassed about using it? And why does God lay the weight of redemption on a man whose voice in some sense fails him?

"DEEP CRIES UNTO DEEP"

Sheer voice, without words, plays an uncanny role in communication.[7] In the biblical narrative of creation, ". . . the earth was without form and void, and there was darkness upon the face of the *tehom*—the *murmuring* deep. And God said, Let there be light" (Gen. 1:2). In this translation, the watery deep is full of *murmuring;* God's first word interrupts a *murmur*, neither speech nor silence.[8] The English *murmur* amplifies the complex harmonics of the Hebrew *tehom* (usually translated simply as "deep"). These include the roots, *hamah, hamam*—hum, murmur, coo, reverberate, roar, growl, groan, stir, rush, tumult, sound of a great throng.

Slavoj Žižek suggests that something beyond silence precedes Creation. Before the first word of the world, there is a background noise, desolate, alien, full of potential life, but lacking in form or meaning. When God first speaks, then, He *creates silence:*

> The primordial situation, then, is not Silence (waiting to be broken by the divine Word) but Noise, the confused murmur of the Real in which there is not yet any distinction between figure and background. The first creative act is therefore to *create silence:* it is not that silence is broken, but silence itself breaks, interrupts, the continuous murmur of the Real, thus opening up a clearing in which words can be spoken.[9]

Silence is created as part of speech. Perhaps this preexistent murmur is what the voice—as yet unchanneled into speech—comes to express. The "murmuring deep" evokes an inexpressible vitality, excessive, vulnerable, intrusive.

In human experience, this murmur is audible in the primal communication of the human voice, seeking out, in singular and common human experiences, the companion depths in the other. "Deep calls unto deep . . ." *Tehom el tehom korei . . .* (Ps. 42:7).

In this sense, Alphonso Lingis argues, the message is not simply what can be *extracted* from the background rumble of the voice. Rather, it includes the noise internal to the utterance, the tone, the rhythm, the cadences, the stammering—all that seems to offer resistance to the pure message.

> We appeal to the others to help us be at home in the alien elements into which we stray: in the drifting and nameless light and warmth of infancy, in the nocturnal depths of the erotic, and in the domain of dying where rational discourse has no longer anything to say.[10]

In our deepest aloneness, we listen for the elemental in each other's voice—which, strangely, is also the particular sound of the other. He is unknown to me; it is her unknownness that I draw on, to help me be at home in the alien elements of my own world.

Stephen Frosh draws on Žižek and Lingis to suggest that this elemental murmur is precisely what reaches across the margins between people and constitutes what Lingis calls "the community of those who have nothing in common."[11]

Perhaps this voice of the murmuring deep, inhuman, elemental, is what resounds in Moses' voice, the noise internal to the utterance.[12] "There is no speaking," says Lingis, "without stammering, mispronounciations, regional accents."[13] The aim of communication is not to eliminate the stammer, the interference, the "rumble of the world."[14] What God wants of Moses is precisely his stammering voice, as the very ground of communication.

Paradoxically, this background murmur, interrupting lucid communication, may be the very enactment of the "Shechina speaking from out of his throat." Emerging from carnal existence, the human voice echoes with the life of things: "sighs, gasps, waverings, droning, hissings, sobs . . . moanings, out of which, sometimes, words are shaped."[15] The noise reverberates in Moses' voice, the background deep in the midst of which he speaks.

It is this dimension of his humanity that Moses resists. He is happy to transfer God's words to Aaron, who will utter them in *his* voice. But it is Moses' voice that God wants: "They must hear *your* voice!" Only so will the tone and rhythm of redemption be heard by the others, still involved in their own murmuring worlds.

CRIES AND WHISPERS

What is the particular quality of voice that God solicits of Moses? Perhaps it is, as Lingis suggests, something elemental, unknowable, vulnerable. "God created everything out of nothing," writes the French poet Paul Valéry, "But the nothingness shows through."[16]

The murmuring deep gives voice to those chinks in the carapace of meaning. Such unconscious transmissions are precisely what Moses fears. Messages that seem to misfire, meanings that cannot be fully controlled, scenarios of redemption that are not realized exactly as they were spoken—these are anathema to Moses. Precisely his voice, in all its fragility and power, its whispers and rumblings, its tones and cadences and faltering, is wanted by God.

Without these interruptions, these cloudings of meaning, some essential quality of redemption will be missing. The word *lamah—Why?* (which, as we have noticed, Moses brings into new usage as a protest against God's failed promises) is the Aramaic translation for *tohu*, for the murmuring emptiness out of which God first spoke. The nothingness that shows through in *lamah* questions threatens human meaning. And yet, it is just this *lamah* that constitutes the human.

Unconscious life threatens dignity, the lucidity of language itself. And yet this *lamah* will later inform the radical cry of the

Psalmist: "My God, my God! Why have You forsaken me? . . . My God, I cry by day—You don't answer; by night, and there is no-silence [*lo dumiya*]" (Ps. 22:2).

André Neher writes: *Lo dumiya* (this non-silence) "is the fall of silence into a deeper stratum of nothingness."[17] Beyond both language and silence, this "metasilence" irradiates Moses' voice, gives it a force that God declares essential. Like the force of a whisper, it subverts and translates official meanings. Expressed as *lamah?* it performs a complex tonality.

When Moses cries out *Lamah?* God answers him: "And God spoke (*va-yidaber*) to Moses, and He said (*va-yomer*) to him: I am God" (6:2). The Hassidic master Mei HaShiloach comments: at first, God responds harshly to Moses' provocative tone (*va-yidaber*). But then God intimates, by changing His tone, that His anger is only superficial. *Dibbur* changes to *amira*, which signifies a soft tone—a whisper of reassurance out of which He names Himself by the name of Compassion. "I am God of the Four Letters [known as the Tetragrammaton]."[18]

Here, Mei HaShiloach stages the human experience of the Other who at first inspires fear, which then modulates into a kind of wonder at such otherness. God, it seems, has a complex identity as Anger-Compassion. When Moses encounters this complexity, it brings to light for him something of his own complexity.

In another passage, Mei HaShiloach discusses the troubled human response to what he calls the Attribute of Justice in God's dealings with human beings. By this he means the cruel and incomprehensible events that may befall a person. Such experiences are, in a sense, more easily handled by someone who is not involved in a relationship with God. Because the believer strives to discern God's meaning in whatever befalls him, he is particularly bewildered and angry when God acts inscrutably.

For the nonbeliever, such experiences can be attributed to chance. Intrusions of nothingness, of the murmuring deep, into the life of the believer, however, are unbearable. God's voice becomes unrecognizable. The believer, therefore, is prone to states of resentment against God.

This kind of theological resentment, advises Mei HaShiloach, is toxic to the soul. So God tells Moses, "Say (*Emor*) to the priests . . ."[19] "In a *whisper*," the Zohar translates. "Whisper to the angry believer that God's intentions are always only benevolent. Even though He may behave inscrutably, His intention, *deep down*, is benevolent."[20]

The whisper is the tone, the voice, of something elemental that softens the stridency of theological claims. It hints at the unfathomable, creating a world where divine love may, despite our pain, prevail. A secrecy is acknowledged. This gives depth to the relationship and to the ongoing conversation.

This secrecy—the whisper—informs the central act of prayer: the Amidah prayer is to be uttered "in a whisper" (*b'lachash*). The instruction acts like a musical direction; standing before God, the human being speaks statutory words that are whispered in the intimacy of a particular voice, crying from the deep.

What, then, is the quality of voice, the singular timbre that belongs to Moses alone? In being spoken "for Israel" (*b'shvil Israel*), even his sacrilegious protests have a power that God accepts. Although he has, in a sense, nothing in common with this slave people whom he now must acknowledge as his own, his voice nevertheless, it seems, resonates with a unique timbre. God wants this voice to address the people; only so will their own voices be aroused to an expressive desire.

"There is secrecy in every conversation," says Lingis.[21] Every conversation that persists over time eventually becomes incomprehensible to others. This secrecy is what makes the communication singular; it is conveyed in tone, accidents of speech, stammerings and raspings of voice. It is the answer to the question implicit in the title of the book in which Lingis discusses these matters: what creates the "community of those who have nothing in common"?

In his book, *Remnants of Auschwitz*, Giorgio Agamben quotes Primo Levi on the lacuna in every testimony:[22]

> I must repeat: we, the survivors, are not the true witnesses. . . . We survivors are not only an exiguous but also an anomalous minority: we are those who by their prevarications or abilities or good luck did not touch bottom. Those who did so, those who saw the Gorgon, have not returned to tell about it or have returned mute, but they are the Muslims, the submerged, the complete witnesses, the ones whose deposition would have a general significance. They are the rule, we are the exception. . . . Weeks and months before being snuffed out, they had already lost the ability to observe, to compare and express themselves. *We speak in their stead, by proxy.*[23]

The drowned have nothing to say: the survivor can speak only of his own exceptional experience, which cannot plumb the depths of the catastrophe. "We, the survivors, are not the true witnesses." The figure called the Muslim, the *Muselman*—who is dead already in life—cannot speak for himself. "We speak in their stead, *by proxy*" (my emphasis).

What is meant by a proxy witness? Agamben formulates the paradox in this way: "Whoever assumes the charge of bearing witness in their name knows that he or she must bear witness in the name of the *impossibility of bearing witness*" (my emphasis). Since there is no possibility of witnessing to one's own death, this precisely becomes the burden of the survivor, the "pseudo-witness."

Testimony to a Holocaust is, by the very nature of the event, impossible. The "true" witness cannot speak his own extinction. Bearing witness to that strangled muteness becomes, then, the project of testimony.

Primo Levi testifies to his own ambivalence about the poetry of Paul Celan. He is drawn to it, while comparing it to "an inarticulate babble or the gasps of a dying man":

> This darkness that grows from page to page until the last inarticulate babble fills one with consternation like the gasps of a dying man; indeed, it is just that. It enthralls us as whirlpools enthrall us, but at the same time it robs us of what was supposed to be said but was not said, thus frustrating and distancing us. . . . If his is a message, it is lost in the background noise. It is not communication; it is not a language, or at the most it is a dark and maimed language, precisely that of someone who is about to die and is alone as we will all be at the moment of death.[24]

Here we have complex testimony concerning the effect on communication of what we have called the "murmuring deep." Babble, gasps, background noise, not a language—the universal sounds of the dying. This is the *na'aka*, the death-groan of the Israelites for whom Moses speaks. This, for Primo Levi, is the tenor of Celan's poetic voice. It enthralls us, but it robs us, frustrates and distances us. It is not communication, he claims, only to qualify his own claim: "or at the most it is a dark and maimed language." In the end, he even acknowledges precisely the human commonality of such language; Celan gives voice to a mortal solitude beyond language.

As Agamben points out, Primo Levi had already attempted to listen to the "inarticulate babble" of a child survivor, in the days following the liberation of Auschwitz. This child, whom the deportees call Hurbinek, emits inarticulate sounds; he is paralyzed from the waist down

> . . . but his eyes, lost in his triangular and wasted face, flashed terribly alive, full of demand, assertion, of the will to break

loose, to shatter the tomb of his dumbness. The speech he lacked, which no one had bothered to teach him, the need of speech charged his stare with explosive urgency.[25]

Everyone in the camp, speaking all the languages of Europe, tries to interpret a repeated sound that Hurbinek utters. But it remains secret: "No, it was certainly not a message, it was not a revelation; perhaps it was his name." Hurbinek dies, "free but not redeemed. Nothing remains of him: *he bears witness through these words of mine*" (my emphasis).[26]

Every act of testimony—perhaps "every word, every writing," declares Agamben, engages, in this sense, with something to which no one has ever borne witness: "This is the sound that arises from the lacuna, the non-language that one speaks when one is most alone, the non-language to which language answers, in which language is born."

In a sweeping movement, Agamben describes the meaningful use of words as precisely that which expresses what was inexpressible. The "true witness" is dead, or in the throes of dying. All he or she has is the *na'aka*, the death-babble that is the failure of language. But the survivor too cannot bear full witness. "Language, in order to bear witness, must give way to a non-language, in order to show the impossibility of bearing witness."[27] It takes two, then, to bear witness: a dialectic of two impossibilities—that of the survivor and that of the Muslim, that of the pseudo-witness and that of the "complete witness."

Agamben carries the paradox of speaking by proxy, on behalf of another's speechlessness, a step further. Normally, one might say that the survivor bears witness to the fate of the dehumanized, dumbstruck victim. But if "we speak in their stead, by proxy," this means that, in some way, the one who truly bears witness in the human is the inhuman: "It means that the human is none other than the agent of the inhuman, the one who lends the inhuman a voice." The survivor lends the true witness a voice, but the survivor has nothing of his own to say. "Testimony takes place where the speechless one makes the speaking one speak." Every testimony, therefore, is a "field of forces"; what it says is that "human beings are human insofar as they bear witness to the inhuman."[28]

Agamben is not indulging in word games. If Moses is acknowledged by God for "speaking on behalf of Israel," this can be understood as discovering in himself a passion to be present, to bear witness, precisely to the death cries of Israelites, his brothers, with whom he as yet has, socially and culturally, nothing in common. For testimony to take place, the speechless ones must make the speaking one speak. Without Moses, they die immured in a tomb of dumbness, like the child Hurbinek. But, even more, without them, Moses has *experienced* nothing to speak of.

Moses' encounter with the *na'aka* of his brothers exposes him to that elemental ground of being that murmurs from the deep. Speaking in their stead, by proxy, he strains against the limits of language. He addresses God in a language, a tone, new to the biblical text: "*Why* have You done evil . . . ?" *Why?* The firm sense of subjectivity of the young Egyptian prince comes into question: "*Who am I?*" (3:11). He must acknowledge his kinship with those who have seen the Gorgon.

In this sense, as Agamben puts it, "Every creator is always a co-creator." Moses lends his voice to the inhuman; only thus, completed by the one who cannot bear witness, will he himself become capable of serious speech. This paradox constitutes the "intimate dual structure of testimony."[29]

When Moses protests to God on the people's behalf, he speaks for an elemental human fragility of which God, apparently, has no knowledge: "What do You care about those who are immured . . . ?" He represents those who are both radically different from him and radically one with him. Redemption, like a complete language, may be impossible. But, if its impossibility is fully realized, it may yet come alive. Where words fail, Moses, the pseudo-survivor, may stammer on their behalf—*b'shvil Israel.*

This moment, when Moses encounters the uncanny strangeness of his brothers' cries, opens him to the agitation of being human. He becomes a stranger to himself and thus a brother to his brothers. What began with a moment of personal exodus, when he left the palace and "went out to his brothers, to see their suffering" (2:11), evolves into a new awareness of his own strange intimacy with their cries.

In the beginning, there was an impulse to witness the suffering of those who are, in consciousness, not yet his brothers. He will make them his brothers by bearing witness. After his flight to Midian, after he has suffered his own death threat, God tells him that his *voice* is necessary, in all its inadequacy, to speak *to* the people, as well as *for* them. No matter what language he speaks, the community of Israel needs his voice.

BIRTH INTO LANGUAGE

Slavoj Žižek writes about the experience of trying to understand a word in a foreign language:

> [We] really understand it only when we perceive how our effort to determine exhaustively its meaning fails not because of the lack of our understanding but because the meaning of this word is incomplete already "in itself" (in the Other's language). Every language, by definition, contains an aspect of openness to enigma, to what eludes its grasp, to the dimension where "words fail."[30]

Reared in the majestic clarity of the Egyptian language and culture, Moses is moved by his encounter with the broken cries of the Israelites to a realization of his own "out-of-jointness."[31]

As he becomes fully present to the ruptured voice of his brothers, something shifts in him. He speaks for them, bringing his own lack to bear on theirs.

From this perspective, there is always something strange, uncanny about human language, a blind spot that is only covered up by the many meanings of words. The sixteenth-century Jewish philosopher and mystic Maharal reads a classic Talmudic passage to suggest something of this inherent lacuna, as well as to place Moses in relation to it:

> The Sages said (B. Niddah 30b): When the newborn emerges into the air of the world, an angel comes and strikes it on the mouth and makes it forget the whole Torah. Why does the angel strike it on the mouth? For it is by way of the mouth that the newborn becomes a living, speaking human being; and by the same blow on the mouth, the angel makes the infant forget the whole Torah.[32]

Maharal goes on to explain that it is through the mouth —through language—that the newborn becomes a complex physical-spiritual being. Before the child is born, it is pure soul, unattached to body, and knowing "the whole Torah." Its creation as a speaking, living human being is completed only after the angel has struck it on the mouth, at the same moment making it forget its previous oceanic soul-existence and opening it to language. Now the child is fully born into the complex human reality. He cites the classic Aramaic translation of Onkelos: "'Man became a *living being*' (Gen. 2:7): he became a living, *speaking* being."

Language, then, constitutes the human being; at the same time, it represents a *loss*. The child loses its pre-human "total knowledge"; the angelic blow obscures and diminishes a primal oceanic harmony; but at the same time opens the mouth of the newborn. A full, complicated being is now born. Embodied soul, he or she bears the insignia of an extraordinary loss that is also an extraordinary gain. Immaculately made, the newborn must suffer a split, precisely in the place of the mouth. Impossible knowledge and embodied voice struggle to testify. The child begins to speak the "out-of-joint" language of an incarnate spirit.

The most striking part of Maharal's reading is its ending. Here, Maharal uses the Talmudic myth of human creation to explain Moses' speech defect. Moses, he declares, remains mysteriously untouched by the angel's blow. His being has never been diminished and evolved in the way the myth describes. He retains a pristine access to "the whole Torah." In him, language is undeveloped; he is, in a sense, not fully born to language and to ordinary humanity.[33]

Maharal here conveys a "secret" understanding of Moses' state as nonspeaker. He is unhindered, undiminished, and therefore, in a sense, not fully human. He has not yet entered the midst of life. When, therefore, Moses speaks of his own inadequacy as speaker, he increasingly becomes aware of a need to enter into the world of language. If he is to speak *to* as well as *for* his newly acquired brothers, he must be born into loss. Purity of being must give way to the possible embarrassments of language. If he is to be *with* the Israelites, he must surrender to the incompleteness of a human life. In this way, perhaps, his people will hear him, as one hears one of one's own kind.

In the biblical text, we can trace Moses' development in this direction. One indication is the way his language becomes more expressive each time he returns to the subject of his speech defect. Increasingly, he becomes aware of *lacking* something he now desires. At first, at the Burning Bush, he describes himself as "not a man of words," a neutral observation. Then, he is "heavy of mouth, and heavy of tongue"—a more sensual depiction of a burden, an excess impeding the flow of language.

Only after he has begun to fulfill his mission—speaking to Pharaoh to no avail, and then to the Israelites, also to no avail

(Ex. 6:9)—does his language erupt in the grotesque imagery of "I am of uncircumcised lips!" (6:12, 30). A foreskin closes his lips, so that they are webbed shut. The movement, somewhat comic, of the mouth compulsively opening and closing, is alien to him. He is whole, singular, and contained in his knowledge of "the whole Torah."

Increasingly, Moses articulates a fantasy of *in-fancy*, of being sealed against language. In reality, of course, he speaks whenever necessary. But, in his own mind, perhaps, there is a desire and a fear—a desire to remain in a state of pristine oneness with the divine, and a fear of being permeable, volatile, fully born.

Perhaps he recognizes in himself something of the impassive dignity of Pharaoh, whose apertures are sealed, who neither listens nor, increasingly, speaks, when Moses makes his demands. As the midrash evocatively puts it, "Pharaoh neither takes in nor gives out." He is never seen either to eat or to excrete.[34] Denying his human needs, his existence in the rhythms of human time, Pharaoh constructs himself as the emblem of an illusory self-possession, as immune to others as he is to his own needs and to the life and death within him. As Rashi says, "He makes a god of himself."[35] A perfect circle, like the mythic Uroborus, the snake with its tail in its mouth, he is impermeable.[36] "I am my river, and I have made myself," he declares in the words of the prophet Ezekiel (Ez. 29:3).

When Moses confronts Pharaoh, he recognizes his own impenetrable condition. To express a new ambivalence, he uses the repulsive imagery of a foreskin sealing his lips—an excess, a "too much" of total knowledge. "Less is more": the foreskin is to be removed, a blockage cut away, so that Moses can gain access to his own vulnerable humanity. Only so will he gain access to his new brothers' hearing. A desire is born—a desire to be born into language, with all its inherent losses.

The point of contact between Moses and the Israelites is Moses' mouth. If his voice is to be heard, he must undergo a trauma, a wound, or a belated blow with no angel in sight. In the meantime, he is in the grip of ambivalence. He wishes to speak, but he refuses to lend his full *voice* in all its elemental force, its unmanageable background noise, to his intercourse with his brothers.

An act of circumcision is apparently required, in order to bring into view Moses' own humanity, blind spot and all. Perhaps the strange and violent scene in chapter 4 of Exodus, where Moses is attacked by God, symbolically expresses this requirement.

On his journey back from Midian to Egypt, at a *malon*, a hotel, God seeks to kill Moses. In this cryptic narrative, Moses is saved from death by his wife, Tzippora, who takes a flint and cuts off her son's foreskin. This mysterious crisis is resolved by an act of circumcision—performed by a woman. Something is staged that speaks of the feminine, of a movement "downwards" into the body and its openings, into the vulnerability of the male organ and of the parted lips that can speak.

This is an act of *milah:* the Hebrew word for *circumcision* evokes the later Hebrew word for *word.* It is echoed in the word *malon* (hotel), which contributes to the verbal field of therapeutic openings, of the operations necessary for human communication. It is after this narrow escape that Moses speaks of himself as "of uncircumcised lips." The physical intervention that has saved his life reminds him of another area of resistance.

SERIOUS SPEECH

In one of his later works, Samuel Beckett describes a kind of visionary experience: "The vision, at last. . . . What I suddenly saw then was this, that . . . the dark I have always struggled to keep under is in reality my most—" Later, he claimed that this "dark he had struggled to keep under," he now saw as the source of his creative life: "Then I began to write the things

I feel."[37] Strikingly, Beckett cuts short the sentence that describes his artistic breakthrough. To put into words "my most—" would be to vulgarize it, to cover over with words its essential elusiveness.

Moses and Beckett make strange companions. But what is in common between those who have nothing in common is perhaps simply the moment of acknowledgment that the "dark," the murmuring deep, is indeed the ground of human being. If Moses is to speak in his own voice as God desires, so that he can *speak for God*, he must lend himself to speaking for that in Israel which he encounters in his own depths. God has let him know—"They must hear your voice!"—that he is not to be a neutral recording device for the divine words. His voice must be faithful to itself, if something of permanent value is to be achieved.

In another modern work, Stanley Cavell writes:

> Writing—heroic writing, the writing of a nation's scripture—must assume the conditions of language as such; re-experience, as it were, the fact that *there is such a thing as language at all* and assume responsibility for it—find a way to acknowledge it—until the nation is capable of serious speech again.[38]

Discussing the birth of the American nation, Cavell points to the need for the "serious speech" that alone can create a national tradition. This serious speech must "re-experience," become newly alive to "the fact that there is such a thing as language at all." In a sense, the heroes of a new nation—the poets who are to rescue language from its exile—must live through the impossibility and the necessity of language. Their speech must be inspired by conviction; its words must carry weight. The written word, especially, must demonstrate "that a particular man put it there."

Moses, born of two cultures, experiences for himself the elemental movement that issues in language. A process leading from the preverbal to the verbal is belatedly lived through in full consciousness. In this way, his difference from his people—his access to the larger knowledge that makes language redundant— makes space for the force of his own particular life, and of the language that expresses it.

The paradox of singularity and solidarity is enacted throughout Moses' life. Sefat Emet articulates the paradox in one of his teachings: "The children of Israel did not listen to Moses because of exasperation and harsh labor" (6:9). His words are inaudible to them—For what purpose, then, does God command him to communicate with them?

Cutting across the stark opposition—either they hear him or his words fall on deaf ears—Sefat Emet frames a third, liminal area, where the people do, after all, register a *trace* of Moses' meanings, though much of the message is obscured. This sense of having lost the large part of a communication creates its own retrospective desire. At a later stage of the redemption process, these vestiges will fill out to retrieve the lost message.

In this Hassidic teaching, Moses' message of redemption is at first largely beyond the range of the people's sensibility. But it does not fall on deaf ears: something is unconsciously imprinted in their minds and memories. Later, it develops and emerges into consciousness. As Christopher Bollas puts it, there is what we think we know; and then there is "what we know but may never be able to think." This is the "unthought known."[39] Sefat Emet is more optimistic about the possibility of an eventual retrieval of the lost message. Consciousness is a process. In the meantime, the unthought known is, in a sense, held in trust by God.

Moses' role in this drama of delayed communication is to express his solidarity with the people by trying—and failing—

to speak. For this, his *voice* is required: only so, will the impress of his being—both foreign and familiar—leave its mark. In this liminal space, Moses too becomes more aware of his absent voice. For him, too, a process is needed.

The nature of this process is perhaps best summed up in the singular description the Torah gives of him: "Moses was very *humble*, more than any human being on the face of the earth" (Num. 12:3). The Hebrew formulation—*kol ha-adam*—suggests not simply that he was the humblest man, but that his humility transcended the human range. Moses' essential difference from the whole of humanity lay in his "humility," his *anava*.

Moses is in fact the only individual in the Bible to be described in this way.[40] Perhaps this refers to his social situation as well as to a moral dimension of his life. Because of his ambiguous origins and his solitary encounter with God at the Burning Bush, he has no social standing among the people. He has no clear position in the class structure. He is both inside and outside, anomalous.

Victor Turner discusses the symbolic values that societies find in such figures:

A rich mythology has grown around the poor . . . ; and in religion and art, the peasant, the beggar, *harijan*, Gandhi's "children of God," the despised and rejected in general, have often been assigned the symbolic function of representing humanity, without status qualifications or characteristics. Here the lowest represents the human total, the extreme case most fittingly portrays the whole. In many tribal or preliterate societies, with little in the way of stratification along class lines, structural inferiority often emerges as a value-bearer whenever structural strength is dichotomously opposed to structural weakness.[41]

Moses as *anav* carries some of the associations of the "lowest" that Turner points out here. In addition to his enigmatic origins, his difficulty with language also sets him outside the intelligible structures of his people. This "weak position," as Turner argues, has a paradoxical strength as a symbolic "valuebearer." It comes to represent the "human total" (*kol ha-adam*, the human essence), which Turner terms *communitas*, and which stands in opposition to social structure:

> . . . from the standpoint of structural man, he who is in communitas is an exile or a stranger, someone who, by his very existence, calls into question the whole normative order.[42]
> . . . In human history, I see a continuous tension between structure and communitas, at all levels of scale and complexity. Structure, or all that which holds people apart, defines their differences, and constrains their actions, is one pole in a charged field, for which the opposed pole is communitas, or anti-structure . . . representing the desire for a total, unmediated relationship between person and person.[43]

In rabbinic discussions of Moses' *anava*, his singular outsider status, lacking language and a place within the structures of the Israelite world, associates him with God, who is willing to abandon His privileged place in the highest heavens and to descend to live among the poor and downtrodden:

> R. Yochanan said, Wherever you find God's power there you find His *anava*.[44] This is written in the Torah, repeated in the Prophets, and once more in the Writings. . . . In the Prophets, it says, "Thus says He who forever dwells high, aloft, whose name is holy" (Isa. 57:15). And later it says, "Yet with the contrite and the lowly in spirit . . ."[45]

God's power is inseparable from His "humility." As Shmuel Lewis suggests, the value associated with this divine involvement with humanity represents the class-less dimension of communitas, affirming the value of the human in itself.[46] Beyond all distinctions, idiosyncratic, particular human beings are connected with one another through their direct association with God. "Anyone who is *anav*, lowly, will ultimately bring God to dwell with the human on earth."[47]

The foundation of human value lies in God's love for sheer, mere humanity, as represented by the "lowest," the exile, the stranger. This "anti-structural" position belongs to Moses, the quintessential *anav*. Like God, he subverts norms. In a sense, he arrives "out of the blue" into the Israelite world, bearing God's word and haunted by his own difference.

"They will not believe me! They will not listen to my voice!" (Ex. 4:1) he protests at the Burning Bush. In the event, the people do believe him (4:31), but they do not listen to him (6:9). In the complex encounter between them, he is from the outset unfathomable. And he continues to be, in a profound sense, "unheard" by them, unknown. The paradox is that it is just through this enigmatic dimension of his being that he is to "bring God to dwell with the human on earth."

Moses' task, then, is to live out his *anava* to the fullest. This will involve an act of "circumcision" that will open up the movement of language between him and his people. In this way, he will become aware, as others cannot, of the bare reality of language and of how it emerges from within the voice.[48] Aware that he needs to speak, he will position his singularity so that it can, after all, both speak to his people and make them speak.

3

Moses Veiled and Unveiled

THE MAN Moses ascends to the summit of the mountain. Before the eyes of those down below, he disappears into thick cloud and consuming fire. The man Moses is responding to a call from God: "Ascend the mountain toward Me!" (Ex. 24:12). Solitary, he ascends; he is lost from view. He approaches the voice from within the cloud and the fire.

Again and again, Moses recedes from the human world below and returns to it. Again and again, he emerges from the darkness where God is (20:18). Just before the event of the Ten Commandments, God expressly summons him in order to send him down and away: "Go on down [*Lech red*], warn the people" not to ascend the mountain in the moment of Revelation (19:21–23). While Moses is at the foot of the mountain with his people, God descends onto the mountaintop and speaks the Ten Commandments.

Forty days later, the man's movement of "up" and "down" takes a tragic turn when he is again summarily dismissed from the heights: "Go on down [*Lech red*]," God tells him; "for your people whom you have brought up from the land of Egypt have acted basely" (32:7). Echoing His previous dismissal before the Ten Commandments, God firmly returns the man to his human context:

> R. Elazar said, God said to Moses: "Go on down from your greatness. Did I give you greatness for any purpose other than for the sake of Israel [*b'shvil Yisrael*]? Now that Israel has sinned, what are you to Me?" Instantly, Moses' strength ebbed so that he had no strength to speak.[1]

Harshly, Moses is ejected from a sublime place that is an inward place. He belongs with his people, down there, out there, far from his essential self. The downward movement represents a sacrifice of his intimacy with the divine. He must "go down" toward a people who are and are not his; he must ground his being in that which is not God. His greatness will emerge only from that position with and for his people.

The shuttle movement up and down represents, then, Moses' trajectory between the human and the divine. In this case, it is the Golden Calf that draws him back down and out to the base of the mountain, where he sees the Calf and the dancing worshippers, and smashes the stone Tablets inscribed by the finger of God. Again, he ascends upward and inward; this time, when, after eighty days, he rejoins the people with a new set of Tablets, he bears on his face the mark of his communion with God:

> And it was when Moses came down from Mount Sinai—the two Tablets of Testimony were in Moses' hand as he came down the mountain—Moses *did not know* that the skin of his face was radiating light from speaking with Him. (34:29)

For the first time in his many descents, the reader is told, twice, that his people "see" him (34:30, 35). Apparently, the scene is presented from their perspective. Something of his interiority radiates from the skin of his face. His visual impact on his people at first distances them from him. Then, he calls them and gradually all come close while he speaks to them.

It is striking that we learn of his singular radiance only in the context of his unawareness. This too, perhaps, becomes part of the people's vision. Through his *not-knowing*, he transforms their field of perception: they fall back. Only later, when presumably he realizes that his private experience is inscribed on his skin, does he *speak* to them in such a way as to draw them close.

At this point, he veils himself. The word *masveh* represents some kind of camouflage, a mask, a veil, a medium that affects the seeing eye. This, we are told, will cover his radiant face at all times when he is not speaking either with the people or with God. Only in these essential encounters, withdrawn within himself and in communion with others, will he be "face to face," bare-skinned.

However, the biblical text describing his practice seems to contradict itself. He covers his face when he finishes speaking with the people and bares it when he speaks with God, *"until he emerges:* when he emerges and speaks with the people, they see his shining face; then he covers his face again until he comes to speak with God" (34:34–35). In this rather cumbersome account, it seems that his face is exposed *only until* he finishes speaking with God. On first reading, we assume that he veils his face at that point and that the people are not exposed to it— which turns out not to be the case. Only after he finishes speaking to them does he replace the veil.

The site of ambiguity is Moses' communion with the people. He is then both veiled and unveiled. The nineteenth-century commentator Ha'amek Davar offers an imaginative reading of the passage. Are there perhaps three positions of the veil, rather than two? When Moses speaks with God, the veil is removed; when he emerges into the social world, it is replaced —but folded back on his head! In this way, the people can see his radiance in the moment of teaching. At other moments, the veil is unfolded to cover his face.

This practice of veiling and revealing represents something of the tension of revelation itself. In order to teach what he has learned, in order to act *for the sake of* his people, Moses must relinquish something of his inner life. A sacrifice is called for in order to establish his relation with the people that alone justifies his communion with God. At the same time, he must speak of and from that inner life.

Here begins his essential role as Moshe Rabbenu, Moses our Teacher. In this role, his words must be spoken in the light of his inner communion with the divine. The skin of his face expresses the physical fragility of the boundary between inner and outer. Expressive of inner states, and vulnerable to external impingement, the skin betrays one's privacy. But the teacher's face is an integral part of the teaching experience. Thus he folds back the veil so that his students will look at his face.

In later times, the sages will recommend that one should look at one's teacher's face as (s)he speaks. They derive this notion of the face as a pedagogical medium from Isaiah 30:20: "And your eyes shall see your teacher's face." Here, Moses "folds up" the veil, because he *desires* the *desire* of his people to see his face at this first fully pedagogical moment.

In his arresting reading, Ha'amek Davar sheds light on the ways in which the human face, in the image of God, expresses nuanced meanings and engages with the yearnings of those who listen to words of Torah. Moses *desires* to draw their eyes to the subtleties of the unsaid, of the implicit, or the ironic, that may be registered fleetingly but powerfully in facial gesture. In this foundational moment, his listeners will be drawn by the singular glow of a face that has been in direct communion with God. Like the light of the sun, this glow has an erotic force. Later generations of students will already know that the teacher's face, even if he has not attained such communion, has much to offer them.

By speaking of desire, Ha'amek Davar places us firmly within Moses' perspective. Moses is moved by a desire to be known, even if this involves sacrificing the intensity of his inner life. There emerges a portrait of Moses the man who reveals himself and veils himself; and of Moses the teacher whose inner world is partially exposed in the space between open and closed, between known and unknown, between inward and outward being. This is an erotic space, traversed by eye beams and rays of light. The folded-back veil communicates a moment of exposure, already framed by its own darkness. In some Hassidic readings, in fact, the veil is simply the appearance of "normality," behind which Moses can pursue his inner life.

THE HALF-OPEN DOOR

The tension of inner and outer, of open and closed, evokes Gaston Bachelard's image of the *half-open door.* Against the logical proposition that a door must be either open or closed, he suggests a formula of poetic imagination:

> Man is half-open being. . . . The door is an entire cosmos of the Half-open. In fact, it is one of its primal images, the very origin of a daydream that accumulates desires and temptations: the temptation to open up the ultimate depths of being, and the desire to conquer all reticent beings.[2]

At times, a door is sharply closed; at others it is wide open.

> But then come the hours of greater imagining sensibility: when so many doors are closed, there is one that is just barely

ajar. We have only to give it a very slight push! The hinges have been well oiled. And our fate becomes visible. . . . Por-phyrus wrote: "A threshold is a sacred thing."[3]

Memories of Bluebeard's chamber evoke

doors that should never have been opened. . . . Or . . . that should not even have been imagined open, or capable of opening half-way. . . . If one were to give an account of all the doors one has closed and opened, of all the doors one would like to re-open, one would have to tell the story of one's entire life.[4]

Moses' practice with the veil can be imagined in a similar way. From the perspective of the people, Moses' radiant face is revealed to them in a "half-open" moment—they see the rays, but the veil is folded ready to descend. The effect, as Ha'amek Davar stages it, generates desire—desire to see and to hear the words of Torah emerging from that light. In fact, he suggests, this is Moses' desire—precisely to evoke in them a passion for seeing the face of the teacher. Like all veils, Moses' veil hides in order to reveal. The half-open door is erotic. Bachelard quotes a French poet, Jean Pellerin: "La porte me flaire, elle hésite" ("The door scents me, it hesitates").

A half-revelation generates the desire for *dibbur*, for language. Strikingly, the word *dibbur* occurs seven times in this short passage (Ex. 34:29–35). Face and language are intensified to create a field of awe and desire. Overcoming their original dread, the people are drawn to hear Moses' words. Still haunted by the Golden Calf, Moses and the people speak face to face.

DEFLECTED VISION

What is the origin of these rays of light? Rashi's answer is "from the cave."[5] The cave is that "crevice in the rock," where God had placed Moses in a moment of greatest intimacy:

And it shall be when My Glory passes by, I shall place you in a crevice in the rock, and I shall cover you with My hand until I have passed by. And I will remove My hand and you shall see Me from behind. But My face shall not be seen" (33:22–23).

Rashi's source-midrash visualizes the divine hand as leaving an imprint of light on Moses' face. Moses had asked to see God's Glory. God's answer had been enigmatic: "You cannot see My face, for no man may see Me and live" (33:20). Now He completes His answer by placing Moses in a cave from which he will indeed be denied his desire. His visual perspective will limit him to seeing "from behind": precisely not the divine face that he desires. As a human being, he can see only obliquely; his vision is deflected. Even the crack of light in the cave will be obscured by the divine hand in the moment of passage. Paradoxically, this obscuring, protective divine hand will leave his face radiating a displaced light. It is as though *vision* is reduced to an after-trace, while *touch* leaves its indelible mark.

Moses' face glows with the effect of the half-open door. He has wished to see totally, blindingly, to experience the divine with ultimate clarity. Instead, he sees the divine "back"; partially, obliquely, in such a way as to suggest what is not being seen. One midrashic commentary translates *"My back:* This teaches that God showed him the knot of the phylacteries [on the back of His head]!"[6] This knot, placed at the back of the head, has a tactile quality, as the fingers find the proper position. Moses' imagination is drawn into the scene. A kind of divine obliqueness moves Moses to bring himself to the encounter. The knot (*kesher*) of the phylacteries suggests *connection*, a complex linking of two beings, divine and human, in a relation that is visualized rather than visual.

INTIMATE COLLABORATION

What the people see in Moses' face, then, is the trace of the after-image of a sheathed transcendence. This complex human radiance is both uncanny and strangely attractive. Moses allows his intimate experience to be partially visible, so as to draw his people into the human field of words.

R. Yaakov Leiner, the late Hassidic author of *Beit Yaakov*, discusses this passage. Why, he asks, was Moses granted these rays of light only when he descended with the second set of Tablets? Surely the first set, written solely by the hand of God (31:18; 32:16) would have radiated a more sublime light? But that original revelation could only be *seen*, without being truly *absorbed* by the seer. Beyond full comprehension, that light remained external to Moses. The second revelation—after sin and forgiveness—involved a *withdrawal* of God's presence. When God moves away, writes R. Yaakov, He leaves a trace of light in the void.[7]

R. Yaakov here refers to the kabbalistic notion of God's withdrawal or *tzimtzum*—the constriction of His light that leaves a pregnant space (known as the *chalal panui*) for the human world. R. Yaakov translates the cosmological notion into psychological terms. We are given a portrait of Moses' experience in the cave and of the way in which, strangely, it generates a unique light of its own. Precisely when the glare of revelation is muted, Moses absorbs the light; he becomes aware of a *deepening* of his own being. Like a teacher who wishes to convey knowledge to a student of limited capacity, God conveys only the "sparks,"[8] without fully elaborating on them. It is the teacher's pedagogical passion that affects the student as he senses how much has been held back. Sparks are thrown off and penetrate deep. An excess beyond words becomes part of the teaching.

This is a narrative of spiritual deepening. Like the cave itself, the shadowy inner space within the brilliant surface of the rock, Moses' inner world dilates and intensifies. His desire denied, he must play in the shadow of a transitional space, where God is only residually present. He will emerge as a separate being from that cavity, which both contains him and is contained within him.

Into this mystical frame, R. Yaakov sets Moses' human experience of the divine. Using a homely image, he tells of the problem of conveying to a friend a sensuous experience, like a particular taste in the mouth. Words alone cannot express this; what is needed is the friend's participation in "sweetening the taste"—in imaginatively relishing, savoring what is evoked from within his own experience. The act of *dibbur*, of communication, stages an intimate collaboration.

ADORATIONS

Here, I suggest, the question of idolatry becomes troubling. The apparently separate narratives of the divine Revelation, of the Golden Calf, of the smashing of the Tablets, of the Cave, and of the sporadic epiphany of Moses' face are all meditations on this basic theme. For idolatry is one resolution of the eternal human dilemma of outside and inside: How do we understand the power that a person, or object, or body of knowledge, holds over us? How does a charismatic teacher, an inspiring text, affect us?

Here is Emerson on the subject of majesty outside and inside:

> A man should learn to detect and watch that gleam of light which flashes across his mind from within, more than the luster of the firmament of bards and sages. . . . In every work of genius we recognize our own rejected thoughts; they come back to us with a certain alienated majesty.[9]

All majesty is, in a sense, our own repressed majesty. It returns to us in the work of genius of another, which we recognize finally as a disregarded part of ourselves.

Stanley Cavell suggests that Emerson is here teaching us how to leave off from reading even his own books:

> Think of it this way: If the thoughts of a text such as Emerson's . . . are yours, then you do not need them. If its thoughts are *not* yours, they will not do you good. The problem is that the text's thoughts are neither exactly mine nor not mine. In their sublimity as my rejected—say repressed—thoughts, they represent my *further, next, unattained but attainable self.* To think otherwise, to attribute the origin of my thoughts simply to the other, thoughts which are then, as it were, implanted in me . . . is idolatry.[10]

Allowing oneself to be "implanted" by the thoughts of the other—this is "idolatry." The idol is not the object itself but the projection of a powerful human desire: the desire for the beauty, the wisdom, the energy of the other to impress itself totally on oneself. Such an idol need not need be a statue; it can be an idea, an institution, a text.

In Cavell's "theology of reading," one becomes conscious in the encounter with a charismatic text that it represents "my further, next, unattained but attainable self." The self becomes tensile, imaginative, inspired by the text to recognize the dim shapes of possible evolutions—further, beyond. Like the half-open door, this encounter both invites and intimidates; it is uncanny, strangely familiar.

The specter of idolatry haunts such encounters. In a remarkable discussion of the Golden Calf, a nineteenth-century commentator on the Torah, known as *Meshech Chochma*, argues that any object, however sanctified—the Holy Land, Jerusalem, the Temple, the stone Tablets inscribed by God's finger—is meaningful only in its symbolic expressiveness: to adore such objects is idolatry. Even a charismatic being like Moses himself holds no intrinsic power: he is simply a messenger who stands between the divine and human worlds, carrying to his people divine words.[11]

Here, he declares, lies the "error" of idolatry. The Golden Calf fiasco originates in the people's adoration of Moses himself, who is conceived as in himself fraught with divinity. So great is the human desire to adore that the screen through which the light radiates is worshipped as the source of the light. This failure of perception leads the people to react desperately to Moses' "delay" in returning from the mountaintop: "And the people saw that Moses was delayed . . ." (32:1). They *see* that if Moses fails to reappear, they will have been abandoned by the divine power that is incarnate in him. It is Moses who has brought them out of Egypt, and who has now vanished into the unknown. ("Moses, *the man who brought us up from the land of Egypt*—we do not know what has become of him.") For them, he embodies divinity; in his absence, a substitute object must be found. The Calf serves well; in the culture of their time and place, the calf is a cliché of numinous power, set for adoration.

IDOLIZING MOSES?

The question is: what do human beings make of the symbolic object? Those who *see* it determine whether it does in fact symbolize something beyond itself. In the end, the symbol is meaningful only to the extent that it is well *read*. To divest the symbol of its suggestive power, of its connection with the unknown, is to invest it with a sterile, hectic vitality, which commands banal adoration.[12]

This reading of the "error" of the Golden Calf is sustained through the whole narrative. On the top of the mountain, God informs Moses what has just happened at its base: "Go on down, for *your people, whom you have brought out from the land of Egypt,*

83

have acted basely" (32:7). God's words take on a satirical tone. They bring Moses a dreadful revelation: in his people's eyes, he has become an idol, his charisma symbolizing nothing other than itself. The people have known all too well exactly what they needed. He has failed to represent the infinite, to stir their imagination to thoughts of their "unattained but attainable self." They have inflated him and at the same time vulgarized him.

In his absence, he has been replaced by the even more vulgar fascination of a golden calf: "They have been quick to turn aside from the way that I commanded them. They have made themselves a molten calf and bowed low to it and sacrificed to it, saying: 'This is *your god*, O Israel, who *brought you out of the land of Egypt*'" (32:8). Using the same formula again, God ironically points up the essential problem. Beyond all the rites of idolatry—the actual making of the Calf, the worship and sacrifices—there is what the people are *saying*, what they are thinking: the Calf is the new object of adoration, filling the vacuum left by Moses himself.

Rashi offers a vivid Talmudic reading of the state of the people at this juncture:

> "Moses was delayed": When Moses went up the mountain, he told them, By the end of 40 days, I will return—before the sixth hour of the day [midday]. The people thought that the day of his ascent was part of the count, but he meant forty complete days, including the previous night. [When he failed to appear at the expected time] Satan came and threw the world into chaos, and displayed an image of darkness and deep fog and chaos, as if to say, "Surely Moses is dead!—therefore chaos has come to the world! Moses is dead, for the sixth hour has passed and he has not returned!"[13]

Moses is fatally late. The people *see* his lateness and are thrown into a catastrophic world—satanic, chaotic—the meaning of which is abandonment. How long does it take for them to betray the covenant at Sinai? In Rashi's narrative, all it takes is perhaps a moment past the expected time. So vulnerable do the people feel that they cannot tolerate an instant without Moses' palpable presence. If he is absent, he is dead.

The infant, too, knows such moments of total panic. The mother's absence, under certain circumstances, becomes traumatic. Donald Winnicott describes the infant's experience as one of "madness": "Madness here simply means a *break-up* of whatever may exist at the time of *a personal continuity of existence*."[14] The question is whether the infant can remain connected with the mother in her absence. The infant's distress can be mended if she returns within a subjectively bearable time. Overly long deprivation leaves an indelible wound—the knowledge of "having been mad."

In this clinical description, Winnicott describes the madness of those who are no longer officially infants. In the midrashic account, the Israelites react to Moses' too-long absence with a similar experience of "madness." Their inner sense of a "sane" world is disrupted. If there is something "infantile" about their condition, this constitutes an error of perception, rather than a sin. For Meshech Chochma, their failing is an optical disorder. What they see is a satanic, chaotic world, with no charismatic figure to walk in front of them. They have not been able to bring to bear upon the image of Moses the larger resources of their own fantasy. Moses' image fades fast.

In endowing him with too much power, they have surrendered to their desire for fetish objects. The immediacy with which they replace him with the Calf seems to indicate that it serves the same psychic purpose. Unhesitatingly, they substitute for the man Moses a hackneyed object of adoration.

They know all too well what they want. "They have been quick to turn aside," God tells Moses, ironically. Their instinct to adore the fetish, to endow it with all their own power, is equaled only by the urgency with which they later repudiate it.

PRIMAL PIETIES

Perhaps the most devastating midrashic account of the Israelites' haste is this one:

> Said Ulla: Shameless is the bride who plays the harlot while
> still under her wedding canopy! Said R. Mari the son of
> Samuel's daughter: What verse refers to this? "While the
> king still sat at his banquet, my spikenard gave forth its fra-
> grance" (Song of Songs 1:12). Said Rav: Yet His love was still
> with us, for "gave forth" is written, not "made offensive."[15]

The bride playing the harlot within her bridal canopy enacts a grotesque synchronicity: her wedding and her harlotry
are almost indistinguishable. No time at all elapses; her husband's image instantly fades from her mind. The midrash connects this parable with a verse from Song of Songs ("While the
king still sat at his banquet, my spikenard gave forth its fra-
grance"), and also with a verse from Deuteronomy: "While the
mountain was still blazing in fire" (9:15). While the divine is
still present, the people are already hankering for another love.
In the midst of the Revelation at Sinai, the people move from
one passion to another.

An internal state is recorded here, an intimate betrayal. The
Israelites' hunger for the omnipotent object manifests itself
even while the fire of revelation still burns at Sinai. A feverish
longing begins in the midst of the wedding ceremony. The
Psalmist later recounts the rhythm of this moment: "Quickly
they forgot His deeds; they would not wait to learn His plan"
(Ps. 106:13).

However, this infidelity is strangely pious. Unable to hold
on to their own experience—the very meaning of *inconstancy*—
the people are at the same time described by God as *stiff-necked:*
"God said, I have *seen* this people that they are a stiff-necked
people" (Ex. 32:9). The people may be fickle, volatile: but to
God's eye they seem all-too-constant. The paradox is inten-

tional, provocative. Through all their feverish urgencies runs an intransigence. Compelled by primal pieties, they resist all appeals to reason.[16]

Perhaps, after all, in fantasy, they have never left Egypt, that place of constricted movement and rigid forms? Perhaps their passion is precisely for the known, the stable object whose excitements are predictable? Perhaps the fear and desire of Sinai moves them too far from their center of gravity? Though they respond with words of faith, "We shall do and we shall hear!" perhaps they have from the outset resisted the "difficult freedom" of this revelation?[17]

FLEEING FROM SINAI

A radical possibility about the idolatrous impulse is raised in another midrash:

> "Quickly they have turned aside": R. Shimeon bar Chalafta said, You have taken the wrong path from the very outset. A man on a journey after walking two or three miles may begin to wander from his path in the third, but surely it is not usual for him to stray from the very first mile? This is what God said: "When you intended to sin, could you not have waited until the second or third day, that you had to start on the very first day?" R. Meir said: It did not even take one day, but while they stood at Sinai they said with their mouths, We will do and we will hear!—but their hearts were turned to idolatry, as it is said, "They seduced Him with their mouths, but their hearts were not constant to Him" (Ps. 78:36–37).

The people are off course from the outset. At Sinai, they mouth words of faith but their hearts are attuned to idolatrous music. Implicitly, their way of accepting divine revelation is already out of tune. It is not a matter of *forgetting* the God of Sinai; rather, the quality of their attention compromises the relationship from the beginning. It is as though the human mind

flinches from the difficult freedom offered by the newly revealed God of the ancestors.

Earlier in the same midrashic passage, a group of sages discusses, with strange arithmetical pedantry, the forty-day period
of Moses' absence: how many days did it take the people to go
off-course? One sage proposes, "Eleven days they were *with*
God, and twenty-nine days they were speculating how to make
the Calf." Another sage reverses the count: they were *with* God
twenty-nine days, and eleven days they were speculating how
to make the Calf. Another view has it that one day they were
with God, yet another argues for two days. Finally, as we have
seen, R. Meir arrives at the most radical conclusion: not even
one day! At the very same time that they were standing at Sinai,
they were already, in some sense, on the run.

A darkly comic view of human nature finds expression in
this version of the Golden Calf narrative. It is not a question of
trying—and failing—to hold on to the impression of Sinai. Instead, standing at Sinai is a posture that compresses within it a
quiver, a flinching reflex. *Being with God*, as the Torah records,
is subject to seismic pulsations. They "shudder backwards"
from their position at the base of the mountain: "And the people *saw* the voices and the lightning and the Shofar blast and
the smoking mountain—and the people *saw*, and they shuddered
backwards" (Ex. 20:18). What they see and how they see leads
them to beg Moses to spare them such a direct revelation. Rashi
offers a vivid midrashic reading: under the impact of each one
of the Ten Commandments, they roll back from the mountain
in a wave and then return to their position—twelve miles each
way—which means that "standing at Sinai" involves them in
convulsive rocking movements covering two hundred and forty
miles!

The people's impulse to delegate the experience to Moses
represents a flight toward closure. Sinai is the "half-open door,"
an invitation to "be *with* God," to find a place in which they can

be *with* the divine. Their inability, even for one day, to hold such an open/closed position, represents a dilemma in the spiritual-erotic life of the human being.

Freud had much to say about the erotic dilemma. In *Freud: The Mind of the Moralist*, Philip Rieff gives this account of it:

> Far from being a champion of unbridled sensuality, Freud acutely understood the intimate connection between libertine and ascetic behavior. Both are excesses, deriving from an imperfect emancipation from childhood's insatiable love of authority-figures. . . . Man is a naturally faithful creature: the most inconstant sexual athlete is in motivation still a toddler, searching for the original maternal object.[18]

Rieff quotes Freud: "The original object [is] represented by an endless series of substitutive objects none of which, however, brings full satisfaction." The paradox of inconstancy and fidelity is played out at the beginning of a life and perversely pursued ever after.

FIRE IN THE BONES

It is this dilemma that God presents to Moses at the top of the mountain. "And now, let Me be, that My anger may blaze forth against them and that I may destroy them, and make of you a great nation" (Ex. 32:10). Essentially, God presents Himself as helpless in the face of human perversity. If He is not stopped—"Let Me be!"—He must destroy the people and create a substitute for them. In a sense, God's counsel of despair has in it some of the "madness" that Winnicott attributes to the infant—as though God too is affected by an inability to sustain His imaginative connection to the people. As Kant puts it, "Out of timber so crooked as that from which man is made nothing entirely straight can be built."[19]

God proposes that He will make of this man Moses—son of two cultures and of none—a father, a patriarch like Abraham (who was promised in similar language that he would be made into a great nation). God will act to *make* him, to reshape him into perfect form. Moses will then be free of the burden of a people who are his and not his: rotten timber, of which nothing entirely straight can be made.

But at this moment Moses begins to speak: this is, in a sense, his first real speech. "Moses entreated in the presence of God His God" (32:11). The unusual verb, *va-yichal* (he entreated) is rich with associations: sickness, engendering, a vacuum, the profane. In a remarkable reading, the Talmud describes Moses as standing in prayer until *feverish sickness* grips him: "What is feverish sickness? R. Elazar said, A fire in the bones!"[20]

The Talmud is giving us entry into Moses' inner world as he pleads for his people. We hear the *tone* of his prayer, which issues from the "fire in his bones." He is internally on fire: a fever that commands God's attention. But what is this fire? A brilliant psychoanalytic reading appears in the commentary of Meshech Chochma, whose thoughts on Moses as proto-idolatrous object we have cited. He suggests that at this moment Moses comes to a realization about himself: that the fire of idolatry burns in his own bones. According to a Talmudic tradition, Moses' grandson appears in the Book of Judges, serving as a house priest to a graven image.[21] Perhaps, Moses thinks, this future idolater carries a genetic streak of idolatry from Moses himself? An unconscious desire, repressed in Moses, will come to the surface in just two generations.

This elaborate rabbinic riff on Moses' prayer—it moves from a word (*va-yichal*) to an association, to a further association, involving several different Talmudic proof-texts, to a moment of uncanny insight—has a serious point. Moses prays so passionately for his people because he realizes that he shares with them a tendency to idolatry. This is a moment of self-knowledge, which opens the door to a full solidarity with his people. Even on the practical level, Moses can now authentically refuse the solution that God has offered him. To destroy the people and have Moses engender a new nation would only replicate the idolatrous impulse that flesh is heir to. An intuition about his own nature profoundly links Moses with his people.

One of the implications of this imaginative reading is that Moses' "mouth is opened" by his insight. This rabbinic idiom is taken up in *Meshech Chochma:* even against God's apparent *closing* of his mouth ("Let Me be!"), his new visceral sense of solidarity with his people—involving his very bones—opens him to effective prayer.

Prayer is a function of such openings of the body and the imagination. A classic reading of Moses' prayer, for instance, is found in Rashi's commentary: "Let me be," God says to Moses (Ex. 32:10). "We have not yet heard that Moses had begun to pray for them, and yet God tells him to let Him be! But here God *opened an opening* for him and informed him that the matter depended on him—If he would pray for them, God would not destroy them!"²² Here too God has apparently closed off the possibilities of the half-open door: "Just let Me be and I will destroy them!" Why then does God need to ask for Moses' permission to destroy? Before Moses has said a word, God has implicitly given him an opening (a *pitchon peh*) to plead their cause.

Between God and Moses, the air is full of subtle intimations and ambiguities. As in all language between people, the literal meaning of the utterance may be distant from the speaker's intention. God says, "Let Me be," and Moses hears, "Don't let Me be." God's words, like all words, need to be *heard:* they need human interpretation. If Moses hears only God's manifest meaning, he will be trapped in a kind of idolatry, seduced by minimum meaning. God hints that Moses is to listen differently; or rather that he is to listen as those who are involved in human dialogue listen. He is to allow God's words to penetrate

him in the infinite range of their possibility. He is to understand "in chords." He is to bring his imagination to bear on
what he hears.

The power of prayer, then, is as though discovered by
Moses for the first time. By an act of intuition, Moses acknowledges God's wish to be disrupted: "It all depends on you!" In
hearing overtones in divine language, he will be most truly
with God.[23] How does he know this? Who told him to *hear* in
this way?

"JUST LET ME BE . . ."

Another Talmudic passage raises the question even more
provocatively:

> R. Abbahu said: If this were not written in the text, it would
> be impossible to say such a thing! This teaches that Moses
> seized hold of the Holy One Blessed be He, like a man who
> seizes his friend by his garment and said before Him: Sover-
> eign of the Universe, I will not let You go until You forgive
> and pardon them![24]

Here, Moses interferes *physically*, as it were, with God. In
an audacious metaphor, he seizes God by the lapel and refuses
to release Him until He forgives His people. Violating all theological correctness, Moses assumes outrageous authority. And
R. Abbahu justifies his daring description by, even more out-
rageously, claiming that it is written in the text! "If it were not
written, it would be impossible to say . . ." The formula is used
provocatively to point up precisely what is not written in the
text: a preface to audacity.

But is R. Abbahu so far off the mark when he listens in this
way to what God says: "Now, just let Me be!?" In various midrashic parables, kings, even as they punish their delinquent
sons, call out to their friends, "Don't interfere!" This can mean
just what it says—or just the opposite. Such moments, *written*

in the text, depend on the attunement of the listener—and the reader.

How does Moses know that he is to hear God in this paradoxical way? And how do the Sages of the midrash dare to read in this way? Essentially, they are reading into the text their own interpretive practice. In a later time, after prophecy has ceased, the Oral Law will engage with the text of the Torah in just such a spirit of imaginative attentiveness: acknowledging both the authority of the text and the necessity for powerful human readings. And the Sages will project their sacred practice onto the biblical figure of Moses: he is, after all, *Moshe Rabbenu*— Moses our teacher.

On another level, however, the play with God's meanings takes its authority from the ordinary use of language. If, for the first time, Moses is able to hear God in this way this is because he himself is being born into the human use of language. If he has been "heavy of tongue and heavy of mouth," this now gives him a gravity of self-awareness as he begins to speak.

God's words, like words of poetry, carry infinite resonance. Open and closed, poetic words express the desire to "open up the ultimate depths of being," as well as the desire to "conquer all reticent beings."[25] Moses, in these midrashic meditations, learns something of God's dynamic desire. God hints to him, He "opens an opening" for him. And Moses, in passing through the opening, begins to hear the desire implicit in all language.

The moment, then, represents a kind of response to the idolatrous passion rampant among the people. For now, Moses knows that this passion is latent in him, too. Moses now understands that fetishisms of all kinds, rigid fixations on perfection, on disappointment, and rage, are postures that ask to be released into movement. This allows him to intuit God's true desire, even as He stages relentless fury.

There are many midrashic sources that narrate moments of this kind, when God, effectively, asks for Moses' "help" with the divine mood of rage.[26] Underlying all these unexpected dramatizations of God-and-Moses, there is a fundamental notion of God's being *with* Israel. To be *with* His people means that God is implicated in their suffering and redemption. On the other hand, it also means that Israel is expected to be attentive to divine presence and absence. A half-open door desires human desire.

The Zohar offers an extraordinary reading of this critical moment between God and Moses. Moses responds to God's appeal: "Let Me be!" (*Hanicha li!*) by protesting: "[If I do as You say] all the nations will say that I have killed the Israelites, *like Noah* [who killed his own generation!]."[27] The Zohar reads Noah's obedience to God's commands—to build the ark and save his own family—as an ethical failure. He should have resisted such a self-serving, "idolatrous" demand. Moses hears in the similar structure of God's offer to him—"Let Me destroy them, so that you can survive to father a better nation"—an invitation to *see through*, or hear through, such an offer. He is to collaborate with God in attending to His true desire. God's words open up such a possibility: "*Atta hanicha li—Just be Noah for Me!*" Moses catches the drift of God's intention ("Don't be like Noah!"); he brings his humanity to bear on God's words, rather than making a fetish of them. This is the moment when Moses begins to speak, as though the fate of the world depends on him.

ICONOCLASM

One more fraught moment in the drama is staged at the foot of the mountain. Moses has descended, bearing in his hands the divinely inscribed Tablets. He is perhaps hopeful that he can still install these Tablets in their intended place, in the Holy of Holies, in the Tabernacle yet to be built. Stone Tablets represent fixity, continuity, the uninterrupted presence of the divine word. But, as he approaches the Israelite camp, he *sees:* "And he *saw* the Calf and the dancing, and Moses' anger blazed and he threw the Tablets from his hands and smashed them at the foot of the mountain" (32:19).

What is it that Moses sees that so enrages him—to the point of smashing the very emblem of divine presence? God has already told him about the Calf. But for the first time, he sees the *dancing*—the ring of ecstatic worshippers, unified in their adoration of the object. A joyful wholeness grips the people—and fills Moses with despair.[28] With stark imaginative seeing, Moses registers their abandonment. Suddenly, the Tablets themselves take on the lineaments of the next idol: literally *God-sent*, totally meaningful, lacking readers who will be capable of being *with* God. A totalitarian madness has seized the people. This is the "great sin," of which Moses repeatedly speaks in his reproaches to the people and in his prayers of intercession: it is the unequivocal joy that closes all half-open doors.[29]

So he smashes the Tablets. And, according to a paradoxical midrash, God later congratulates him for his iconoclastic act. Referring to the Tablets "which you smashed" (Deut. 10:2), God implicitly says, "Congratulations [lit., May your strength be firm!] that you smashed them!"[30] Through a play on words, God retrospectively celebrates Moses' most impulsive and disruptive act. This was an inspired act, God says, because it directly engaged with the human passion for idols. By shattering the Tablets before their eyes, Moses breaks the spell of the fetishizing gaze.

For Moses himself, this iconoclastic moment takes on the deepest significance. God has already revealed to him how the people see him: "Your people whom *you brought out of the land of Egypt* have acted basely." God bends His words ironically around the people's view of things. For them, Moses has been first in a series of fetish figures. This realization shocks him into a new consciousness: consciousness of the human need to project, to objectify what is within; consciousness particularly of himself as both the object and, potentially, the subject of such projection. What he realizes is that anything or anyone can be pressed into service of the idolatrous impulse. This would include the God-inscribed Tablets, Moses, or the divine word. Idolatry lies in the nature of the relationship between self and object.

Perhaps Moses himself, bearer of a double identity, leader of a slave people long detached from its own identity, and traumatized first by slavery and then by the rigors of freedom—perhaps he particularly feels the fire in the bones, the wish for the absolute presence of God?

In fact, in the course of the Revelation at Sinai, he and the other leaders had been granted a vision of God: "They saw the God of Israel: under His feet was the likeness of a sapphire brick, like the essence of heaven for purity" (Ex. 24:10). The reader's imagination is stalled by the mysterious detail of the imagery. Did they see the God of Israel? Or merely what was under His feet?

Strikingly, Sifrei reads the "likeness of a sapphire brick" to refer to the Israelite labor with bricks and mortar in Egypt: "Throughout the duration of the slavery, the divine Presence was, as it were, enslaved *with* them."[31] The midrash associates the sapphire brick not with sublime, ineffable realities but with the bricks of Israelite slave labor. God identifies so totally with Israelite trauma—He is *with* them in their suffering—that this identification becomes a dimension of His being.[32] He contemplates the brick and is constantly reminded of Israel's suffering. What Moses and the elders see is that God is implicated in the Israelite history of trauma and redemption.[33]

The effect of this midrash is unexpected. Instead of a vision of the transcendent God, Moses and the elders have seen something of God's associative process, as it were: the process that leads Him to identify with human suffering. In the end, Moses is turned back to himself and his people, to the work of imagination and reflexive consciousness.

Also striking is the description of the brick as only a *likeness—k'ma'aseh livnat ha-sapir.* Not a defined object but an approximation—*like, as though* . . . In a powerful Hassidic teaching, Mei HaShiloach speaks of the provisional, imaginative nature of all human conceptions of the divine. Reading the word *anochi—I—*in the First Commandment ("I am God, your God, who brought you out of the land of Egypt") he points to the letter *chaf,* which differentiates it from *ani,* the other word for *I.* This letter he calls the *chaf* of similarity, the prefix that means "like." As in the vision on the mountain, the divine is to be seen not as something stable, rigidly defined, fully known, but as a process, a becoming, only a likeness, a provisional understanding.

This letter *chaf* represents human limitation and the unfolding human capacity for understanding more and deeper. "If God had revealed Himself as *ani,* that would mean that He fully revealed His light, so that there would be no possibility of going deeper into His words." Today's light will tomorrow look like darkness by comparison with tomorrow's light. Without this *chaf* of approximation, without this awareness of provisional understanding, we would have, essentially, idolatry. God, too, can be pressed into the service of the human desire for the graven image.

In his imaginative, deeply serious play with the letter *chaf,* Mei HaShiloach is really talking about language, its limitation, and the need for God to undergo a *tzimtzum:* to condense the totality of revelation by introducing the provisional, the approximate into the ways He is perceived. The letter *chaf*— shaped like a cave, like a cavity, a hole—is at the heart of God's relation with human understanding. This involves a reduction, a loss—but also invites a process of human *deepening* that is infinite, as He is infinite.

Of course, the letter *chaf* also represents the *imaginative.* In the epiphany at Sinai, God acknowledges human possibilities of perception. He gives the Torah; but the real question immediately becomes one of reception. Human consciousness is constituted by the use of fantasy, which creates worlds of meaning. When truly acknowledged, fantasy can be owned in its power and its peril.

The hazard of idolatry is the wish to have an object perfectly adjusted to our needs. This wish is part of the human experience of Revelation. If God is kept in mind, however, the desire, precisely, for an achieved perfection must be frustrated. In this way, we remain—always incomplete, within and without —hot in pursuit of the infinite.

BEING *WITH* GOD

Moses' most intimate experience of the God of incomplete presence occurs in a "crevice" in the rock of Sinai—in a cave, a letter *chaf* carved into the mountain. "Please let me see Your glory," he had beseeched. God had responded, "You cannot see My face, for no human being can see Me and live. . . . I will place you in a crevice in the rock and I will cover you with My hand till I have passed by. Then I will remove My hand, and you will see My back; but My face shall not be seen" (Ex. 33:20–23).

This crevice in the rock, a narrow place with limited visibility, allows a mere ray of light to enter. This ray—piercing, dense—is absorbed into Moses' face and leaves him mysteriously radiant. Even the word for "crevice," *nikrah*, and the word for "ray," *keren*, are anagrams, enacting the link between Moses' radiant skin and the experience of the Cave. These rays, which at first intimidate and then attract the people, are made of pure desire, an intensity of vision that *sees through* the crack in things.

In this sense, what God offers Moses is both less and more than he desires. The back, not the face: no fullness of divine

presence, but intimations, traces, interpretations that passionately connect Moses with God and His words. What opens up
is the dynamic space of being *with* God.

But this connection involves work, like the "work of the
sapphire brick."[34] If we imagine Moses throughout the course
of the narrative—from God's revelation at the top of the mountain, through Moses' deeper understanding of the meaning of
idolatry, when he sees the Calf and the dancing; through the
shattering of the Tablets and the massacre and plague that follow; to his intensifying prayers of intercession and his second
descent from the mountain, bearing a new set of Tablets—
inscribed, this time, by his own hand—a layered personal tale
unfolds. This is a tale of solidarity with his people, which is
compounded of stark loneliness and the transcendence of self-
pity. By the time he *sees* the Calf and the dancing, he knows
both the people's sin and his own implication in that sin. He
knows that he has played a role in their fantasy life and that
they have ejected him from that role. Symbolically, he has been
destroyed by them, like the fetish that fails to provide the required service.[35] At that moment, he is stripped of any clear
sense of his role as their leader.

Reified by his people, Moses finds a way of speaking about
them that expresses deeper solidarities. He moves from referring to them as "this people," or "Your people," to an imaginative solidarity with them: "Forgive *our* iniquity and *our* sin!"
(34:9). But what sin did Moses commit?

"I saw that you had sinned against God your God"
(Deut. 9:16). He saw that Israel had no leg to stand on, and
he joined his soul with them and smashed the Tablets. Then he
said to God, "They sinned and I have sinned, for I have
smashed the Tablets. If you forgive them, then You can for-

give me, as it is said, '*And now, if You forgive their sin* . . . ,' then You can forgive my sin as well. And if not—if You do not forgive them, then don't forgive me, but rather erase me from Your Book that You have written."[36]

In smashing the Tablets, Moses "joins his soul with them." He finds a place where he can speak *with* and *for* them. He is inextricably bound up with them. The midrash beautifully solves the riddle of the unfinished sentence: "And now, if You forgive their sin . . ." The gap alludes to his own sin, in erasing the Tablets of the Law; this is the unspoken counterweight that Moses has added to the scales of judgment. If God does not forgive, the text continues explicitly, "then *erase me* from Your book" (Ex. 32:32). Poetic justice . . .

The previous passage in the midrash compares breaking the Tablets with the act of a matchmaker who hears reports that the bride has misbehaved. He tears up the marriage document before it can be handed over to the bride. Better, Moses thinks, that she remain ignorant of the severe requirements of the Torah. In doing so, he becomes a kind of accomplice with the bride. By associating himself with her in this way, he can forcefully bargain for forgiveness.

This strange solidarity, expressed through fraught images of wayward brides and ingenious matchmakers, is found in many midrashic texts. What moves Moses through his deliberately outrageous performances is a passion of solidarity that, just in this crisis, surprisingly emerges.

Even more surprisingly, perhaps, God accepts Moses' stagings of reality. By implicating himself with his people in this dramatic way, Moses is, in fact, fulfilling God's command: *Lech red*—"Go on down, for your people . . . have acted basely" (Ex. 32:7). In moving downward, in divesting himself of his "greatness," he joins his soul with them. At the same time, in relinquishing this greatness, he connects himself in a different way with God. All his greatness, we remember, was for his people's sake. "Now that Israel has sinned, what are you to Me?"[37] Rather woundingly, Moses is cut loose from God, at the very moment that he realizes his isolation from his people. Reintegrating the fragments of his identity now depends on him, on his prayers, on his words. In acknowledging a new relationship with his people, he finds a way of being, precisely, *with* God.

WELCOMING THE TEACHER'S FACE

Lech red—"Go on down . . ."—indicates a counterintuitive movement into the world where light comes in rays. This is a world in which much light is withheld; a world of prayer and of study of Torah. Time and change mean instability, uncertainty —and possibility: hence prayer. The study of Torah opens one to one's unattained but attainable inner light. For this reason, when Moses relates to the people the Torah he has learned from God, his face is unveiled, momentarily revealed. It conveys the work of Torah, the intensity of desire. Hinterlands of meaning are evoked by its peculiar radiance.

Strangely, Moses desires that the people should desire to gaze at his face. How is that to be understood? What is the gaze—this reflexive movement, the seer wishing to see the other's seeing—that Moses desires? Surely not the enraptured gaze at the fascinating object, complete in itself—the graven image? But rather the gaze of the student, the face that flickers with its own process of attunement.

Why does Moses desire this gaze? R. Nahman of Bratzlav, the early Hassidic master, quotes a verse from Isaiah as a key to the question: "Your eyes shall see the face of your teacher" (Isa. 30:20). A subtle transaction takes place between teacher and student. Seeing the teacher's face means welcoming it into one's own face, drawing in the light of his/her wisdom into one's own face. Since the face radiates with the particular wisdom of its bearer, an idiosyncratic light transfers from face to face. This is an act of *kabbalat panim:* normally the idiom for "hospitality," the expression is here used literally to refer to the student's active reception of the face of the teacher. In learning Torah, one opens one's face in a profound movement of hospitality. The teacher's face becomes a guest in the inner world of the student. Doors are opened; a deep impress is invited. One expression accepts the imprint of another, and a spiritual "family" is created.

R. Nahman's language is one of fantasy. Faces open to other faces; light radiates and penetrates; a guest enters a host's home. One might call this *metaphoric* language. But this would not do justice to the intimate *realism* of R. Nahman's description. In his version of transference, playful imagery conveys the mystery of *receiving* Torah. The Giving of the Torah (*Matan Torah*) at Sinai quickly opens up to the complexity of Receiving the Torah (*kabbalat haTorah*). From now on, this will be the real issue: What does the student do with what (s)he is offered? The classic response of the people is *"We shall do and we shall listen!"*—a response of obedience and faith. But then the Golden Calf springs whole from the fire, and plays out the implicit hazards of a passive reception of Revelation. To transcend this state, active, imaginative *seeing* draws in the light of the teacher's face.

Emerson, we remember, describes just such a process, by which one comes to acknowledge an internal radiance:

A man should learn to detect and watch that gleam of light which flashes across his mind from within, more than the luster of the firmament of bards and sages. . . . In every work of genius we recognize our own rejected thoughts; they come back to us with a certain alienated majesty.[38]

Rejecting one's own thought, one risks idolatry, which is the fantasy that one can allow oneself to be simply implanted by the thought of the other—the teacher, the text. Rather, one hosts the light of the other so that it irradiates one's own lights and shadows. As Cavell puts it, the thoughts of the teacher are neither exactly mine nor not mine: they represent "my further, next, unattained but attainable self." Without that constant movement of light, desire freezes in place.

What Moses' face offers is the light that originates in the cave, the crevice in the rock. It conveys a depth of experience born of not-seeing, as God's face passes by. The *nikrah*, the crevice, the fissure in the rock, engenders the *karnayim*, the rays of narrowed light. The wordplay expresses the force of such fragmentary light; instead of a dazzled totality, Moses' face knows what it is to live something through to the end.

Virginia Woolf noted that in writing *Mrs. Dalloway* she invented a "tunnelling process": ". . . how I dig out beautiful caves behind my characters."[39] Crevices in the rock limit direct illumination but offer fantastic perspectives of shadow and light. The letter *chaf*, which creates a gap in the *ani*—a space of provisional illumination, like a cave in the rock surface—opens up to an infinite yearning. This is loss, incompleteness, carried deep into the self.

From these moments of encounter between Moses and his people—face-to-face, like his meetings with God—the play of faces generates a learning process. This is a pedagogical moment, and a therapeutic one. Here, *Moses our teacher* (*Moshe Rabbenu*) comes into being. For the student, what would it mean properly to *host* the teacher's face? Cavell puts it beautifully. A complete interpretation—of a text, say—would not be a matter of providing all possible interpretations, but a matter of "seeing one of them *through*." It would mean taking the "risk implicit in the business of reading" texts or faces, of *reading in*, of *going too far*. It would be full acknowledgment of the revelation within.[40]

To see something through, of course, might also mean *seeing through* a façade, a carapace. If Moses folds back the veil of his privacy, the gesture declares that he wants those with whom he speaks to *see through*, to penetrate a conventional surface. He is, in a sense, creating them as hosts of his light. He is imparting something of his own experience in the Cave. He is initiating them into a newly imaginative perception of *dibbur*, of language in its dynamic, shape-changing power. In seeing the traces of God's passing, he had become aware of this power of the spiritual imagination to create the world. Now, he "transfers" this awareness to his people. They absorb its oblique singularity, and their own singularity is awakened.

LOOKING AT THE SUN

In this scene of sevenfold *dibbur*, Moses brings to light the depths of his students. Like looking at the sun, looking Moses in the eye risks blindness. Some indirection, some distance preserves the student from the dazzle of the idol. This is Moses' knowledge from the Cave. He has been preserved from the dazzle by God's hand. In order to stage for others a similar experience—an image, an approximation—he folds back his veil. Like the great artist, he exposes his face—the after-image of an obscured revelation. Like his creator, he wants, to the depths of his being, to be known. But if the knowing can only be partial, fragmentary . . . ?

The artist, say, paints the sun—an image of the sun, a mock sun. This, says J. H. Miller in his discussion of the work of William Turner, is both the highest artistic act—he brings his own sunlike creativity to light—and a "dangerous act of aesthetic sacrilege."[41] He uses pigment that darkens, tending toward mud, challenging the eternally invisible energy of the real sun.

But Turner, in his many suns, often revisited the savage story of Regulus, the Roman general and consul, who was, in punishment for failure, exposed to the sun after his eyelids were cut off. In painting his suns, Miller suggests, Turner was enacting his own power to create a mock sun, an image that would have the same terrible power over the viewer. The paradox of the artist's ambition is to create with earthy materials "not an imitation of light, but a light-source itself."[42]

Here is a description of Turner making a sun:

> He had a large palette, nothing in it but a huge lump of flake-white; he had two or three biggish hog tools to work with, and with these he was driving the white into all the hollows, and every part of the surface. This was the only work he did, and it was the finishing stroke. . . . The picture gradually became wonderfully effective, just the effect of brilliant sunlight absorbing everything and throwing a misty haze over every object. Standing sideway to the canvas, I saw that the sun was a lump of white standing out like the boss on a shield.[43]

"Wonderfully effective," thick gobs of white paint driven by hog tools into the surface—Turner's painting becomes itself an image of the effectual imagination which reshapes reality. Seeing through the lumpy world, his perspective intensifies so that we, too, will see what is, after all, there. Words are the equivalent means at Moses' disposal. They generate rays that are at once God's, his own, and Israel's.

4

◆╺◆╸◆

Moses in the Family: Mirrors and Foils

IN QUEST OF BROTHERHOOD: EARLY HISTORY

The quest for brotherhood and the question of brotherhood pervade Moses' early life. Both father and mother soon fall out of his story. His brother and sister, Aaron and Miriam, however, remain as both foils and mirror reflections. Moses' singularity is perhaps best understood through his relations with those who are closest to him.

It is God who definitively declares Moses' difference from his brother and sister. Addressing their envy of him, God says: "*Not so [lo chen]* is My servant Moses!" (Num. 12:7). Miriam and Aaron and all other prophets are in one category and Moses alone in another. They may experience God in dreams and visions, but Moses alone is "faithful in all My household." His connection with God is of a different order.

The Torah, of course, ends with a similar statement about

Moses' singularity: "Never again did there arise in Israel a prophet like Moses, whom God knew face to face" (Deut. 34:10). But that "last word" of the Torah emerges from some ahistorical point: a view from nowhere. It is a metaphysical statement, detached from subjective experience. In the scene with Miriam and Aaron, however, God enters the family situation in the thick of its emotional embroilment. Moses, He says, is simply other, *lo chen—not so, not like* his siblings, not like any other prophet. His metaphysical difference begins at home, in his own family.

From the beginning, Moses' difference sets him apart. He is the child born after Pharaoh's decree against male babies. From the moment when, at three months of age, he is cast out alone on the Egyptian river, he remains essentially alone. This, even though his sister, who is identified at first simply *as* his sister (Ex. 2:4), stands guard over him and even returns him to his mother's breast. His infant experience, as the child of genocide, shuttled between mothers and cultures, largely obliterates his birth family from memory.

One telling fact is that his parents and sister are unnamed in the early narrative; he is, in fact, the first to be named—by the Egyptian princess—after he is weaned and restored to her. In the beginning, he himself and those who figure in his early life are referred to simply as a man, a woman, a child. Relationship, therefore, and the attribution of relationship become highly significant in this narrative: Moses is repeatedly called a "child," but Pharaoh's daughter recognizes him as "a child of the Hebrews" (2:6). His sister proposes bringing "a woman" to nurse the child "for you"; Miriam summons the "child's mother," who is charged by Pharaoh's daughter, also unnamed and always referred to in this way, with nursing "this child for me" (2:9). The woman takes the child, nurses him, and on weaning him brings him back to Pharaoh's daughter—"And he became a *son to her.*" Her effective maternal right over him is asserted in her naming of the child: "I drew him (*gave birth to him*, in Egyptian) from the water" (2:10).

The passage quietly describes the splitting of identity of a mother's child, whose sister arranges for the ultimate re-mothering of that child, as if he were reborn. Miriam's act is a survival response to the world of violence that is Egypt. When Moses enters conscious life, he "*goes out* to his brothers to see their sufferings" (2:11).[1] This first personal exodus presages the larger national event.

Moses' quest is for brothers, for others who are like him. As we have noticed, it is unclear whether Moses knows the Hebrew slaves to be his brothers. Possibly, the young Egyptian prince, uneasy in his identity, emerges from the palace to look for kin in the least likely place, among the low-caste slaves. He "sees" their suffering, their labors. At the same time, he "sees" an Egyptian—who, like him, belongs to the master race—beating "one of his brothers." The ironies multiply. The narrator refers to the slaves, factually, as "his brothers"; he himself consciously identifies at first with the Egyptian—only to find himself moved toward a sense of kinship with the one who is being beaten. Ambiguously, his brotherhood with the Hebrew slave becomes a subjective choice. It leads him to kill the Egyptian, responding to violence with violence.

Strikingly, this whole early passage of his life is conducted in almost total silence. Without uttering a word, he absorbs the situation and acts.

The following day, the split in identity is further complicated when he sees one Hebrew about to kill another. He cries out—his first speech: "Why would you strike your fellow?" With this outraged cry, he protests against the violence that erupts between those who are like each other, like brothers. Implicitly, he also expresses his own sense of lacking a "fellow." His new sense of brotherhood is complicated as the "guilty one" taunts him: "Are you going to kill me as you killed the Egyptian?" Having disposed of one violent other, he discovers otherness even among the victims of violence. In a kind of "double-bind" situation, Moses is silenced. He says nothing, and flees.

Silent still, he arrives at the well in Midian, saves Jethro's daughters from the shepherds, and marries Tzippora. Then, he speaks by naming his son Gershom, "for he said, I have been a stranger in a foreign land" (2:22). Using both the words for "stranger" and "foreign," he makes a factual observation and a reflexive one. Classically, naming a child is an opportunity for self-reflection. This is Moses' first observation about himself.

Still overwhelmingly silent, Moses arrives at the "mountain of God," where a bush burns without being consumed. Fascinated, in soliloquy, he then says, "Let me turn aside to see this great vision" (3:3). When God calls him by name—twice—he responds, "Here I am!" But throughout God's long speech, in which He promises salvation for "My people," and commissions Moses as His delegate in delivering the Israelites from Egypt, Moses utters only two questions: "Who am I . . . ?" he asks (3:11); and, "If they ask me, What is His name? what should I tell them?" (3:13). Both questions express a desire to know mysteries: his own identity, God's identity; questions within questions. But in both cases, his desire is framed by the need to explain himself to others. His concern, it seems, is largely with how he will be received by Pharaoh and by the Israelites, who now represent fragments of his split identity (his "grandfather," Pharaoh, on the one hand, and his newly perceived brothers, on the other).

Again, Moses listens silently to God's long speech commissioning him and foretelling the narrative of the Exodus. Only in chapter 4, after a scattering of brief questions, does Moses begin to speak his mind: "They will not believe me, nor will they listen to my voice" (4:1). Repeatedly, he speaks of his inability to speak: "Please O God, I have never been a man of words, either yesterday or the day before, or now that You have spoken to Your servant; I am heavy of mouth and heavy of tongue" (4:10). In a sense, he is never as eloquent as when he invokes his speech disability, the weight he carries inside his mouth. Ironically, this is his most expressive moment so far, when he puts something of his inner life into words.

1. AARON

"All brothers hate one another . . ."

Why does he so passionately resist God's call? Rashi diagnoses his resistance as a phenomenon of *brotherhood:* "All this resistance was because he did not want to assume greatness (*gedula*) over his brother, who was older (*gadol*) than him and already a prophet."[2] Reluctant to usurp his elder brother's role in the family and in the community, Moses shrinks from "greatness."

The idea of disrupting the natural order, specifically the law of primogeniture, carries the stigma of a primal taboo. Although there are many violations of this norm in the book of Genesis—the younger brother chosen over the elder—the norm retains power to create a shared world of values and practices. As Robert Cover puts it, it remains "the great fault-line in the normative topology of the Israelites."[3]

So Moses is reluctant to cross that line with his brother Aaron. Hence, since Aaron is the established prophet and leader of the Israelites, Moses for the first time mentions a speech defect that he claims as a longstanding disability.[4] Is this an alibi to release him from God's call? Has he developed this "stammer" in the stress of his new awareness of a complex identity? As we have noticed, his early life has been marked by long periods of silence punctuated by brief convulsive speech made up of questions, negations, and a single, powerful expression of attentiveness: *Hineni!—"Here I am!"* (3:4). A confusion of tongues . . .

In some midrashic sources, his reluctance to usurp his brother's leadership is glowingly praised: "You find that all brothers hate one another . . . [but Moses and Aaron] did not hate one another but rejoiced in each other's greatness."[5] Moses refuses God's call because "all these years, Aaron my brother has been the prophet—should I now trespass on my brother's terrain and distress him!" God then reassures Moses precisely on this score: Aaron "will come out to greet you *with joy in his heart!*" (4:14).

God's plan is to assign the brothers different roles that will honor Moses' sensitivity to his brother's role: "There is your brother Aaron the Levite—I know that he speaks with great ease." Moses will convey God's words to his brother who, as an eloquent speaker, will act as Moses' mouthpiece. This plan is, in fact, carried out, when Moses later meets Aaron (4:27–31). Moses' oedipal anxiety is relieved, and his relation with his brother becomes a model of ideal fraternity.

There are, however, some significant complications in this narrative. First, strangely, when God responds to Moses' unspoken anxiety about usurping Aaron's role, He is described as *angry* with Moses (4:14). Second, in midrashic readings Moses is punished for resisting God: he loses the function of High Priest, which is transferred to Aaron, together with the speaking function.[6] In some way, speaking to Pharaoh will transform Aaron's ritual role. And third, God violently attacks Moses on his return journey to Egypt: "And it was on the road at a hotel that God encountered him and sought to kill him" (4:24). According to midrashic tradition, the reason for the attack is Moses' continuing resistance to God's mission. Even though

God has reassured Moses about Aaron's reaction, Moses still maintains his posture of resistance: "Send by whose hand You will send!" (4:13). And God is angry. Moses' reluctance to *speak*, to assert his power in voice and word, alienates him from God.

The result is a lifelong preoccupation with the issues of language. In this preoccupation, his brother Aaron is deeply involved. On the face of it, the tension between them is allayed; they are to play complementary roles; fraternal aggression, the tragic subject of Genesis, gives way for the first time to brotherly love. And Moses can for the first time speak of "my brothers": "Let me go now and return to my brothers in Egypt, and let me see if they are still alive" (4:18). But whom exactly is he referring to? His siblings Aaron and Miriam? Or the Israelites, whom he now perceives as his kin? The smaller and the larger fraternal groups are no longer objects of such anxiety. That is on the face of it. But even though Aaron has become his brother and his ally in a new and fuller sense, this, apparently, does not entirely resolve the question of Moses' identity. He remains heavy of mouth, unable to speak. God is angry; Moses is punished by losing the High Priesthood; God attacks him on his journey back to Egypt.

In the wake of Freud and other contemporary thinkers, Julia Kristeva claims that language originates in an experience of loss, the loss of "an essential object that happens to be, in the final analysis, my mother."[7] The mourner mourns the lost mother and can then recover her in symbolic language: he can speak about her. "Depressed persons, on the contrary, *disavow* the loss." They can never reach the position of really *losing* and mourning. In consequence, their language has an artificial quality, cut off from vital experience. The condition of *asymbolia*, the loss of symbolic meaning, writes Kristeva, manifests itself as melancholia, a "fundamental sadness." Their language "is to them like an alien skin; melancholy persons are foreigners in their maternal tongue. They have lost *the meaning—the value—of their mother tongue for want of losing the mother"* (my emphasis).[8]

In Moses' early life, his mother is lost, briefly retrieved, and then replaced by another mother, complete with a new tongue. Never does he speak of this loss, or of the double loss, as God urges him back to the brothers and the mother tongue of a primal existence. Only when he speaks about speech, reflexively mourning what he is *not*, does the world of the symbolic begin to open up for him.

The melancholy subjectivity of a Moses is juxtaposed with his brother Aaron's expressiveness. God describes Aaron as *dabber ye-dabber*, as a fluent speaker, who is "coming forth to greet you with a joyous heart." Active, spontaneous, emotionally integrated, Aaron will provide what Moses lacks—he will be Moses' mouthpiece (literally, his *mouth*), while leaving Moses the role of inscrutable divinity, remote, somehow stranded.

With all the complementary harmony of the brothers, each rejoicing for the other, a strain persists in Moses' experience. When, later, Aaron is in fact appointed High Priest in the Tabernacle, Moses' reaction is deeply ambivalent. Many midrashic sources tell of his disappointment at the loss of the priestly role. Since he acts as High Priest during the seven days of inauguration, he slips so totally into his role that he is shocked when God makes it clear that he is merely to *dress* Aaron in his priestly vestments. It is Aaron who will wear those vestments, which in themselves represent expressiveness.

The notion that clothes make the man dominates these biblical descriptions of the priest for whom role and clothes are equivalently effective. The priestly breastplate is set over Aaron's heart, which rejoiced at Moses' leadership. Aaron is a fitting wearer of these robes; an error or omission in these robes would disqualify his service. The harmonious connection between inward and outward, unarticulated thought and representation, the heart and its language, is his territory.

Moses and the High Priesthood

As for Moses, the moment in which he is commanded to invest his brother in the priestly role becomes, in the midrashic tradition, resonant with personal feeling. Suddenly, unexpectedly, there is grievance, a sense of loss, an experience of mourning.

In one expression of this theme, Moses is compared to a displaced wife:

> "And as for you, you shall bring forward your brother Aaron
> . . ." (28:1). It is written, "If Your Torah had not been my play,
> I should have perished in my poverty" (Ps. 119:92). When
> God told Moses, "As for you, you shall bring forward your
> brother Aaron . . . ," *He did him an injury.* God said, "I had
> possession of the Torah, and I gave it to you: if it were not
> for the Torah I should have lost My world!" This is like a
> wise man who married his close relative and after ten years
> together, when she had not borne children, he said to her,
> "Seek me a wife!" He said to her, "I could marry without
> your consent, but I seek your compliance." So said God to
> Moses, "I could have made your brother High Priest without informing you, but I wish you to be great over him."[9]

The analogy involved in this midrash is startling. Moses is compared to a wife who is asked by her husband to find him another wife! When God asks Moses to appoint his brother High Priest, He is similarly *doing him an injury.* We require the shocking analogy in order to appreciate how much pain the divine will causes Moses. God asks for Moses' *invetanut,* his cooperation, his compliance in a move that undermines his own status.[10] A pang of loss initiates him into conscious mourning.

The wife's humility/compliance becomes, in the narrative of God and Moses, a demand that "you be great over him." The apparent dissonance between humility and greatness becomes the central tension of the midrash: compliance, forbearance, will be renamed as greatness. In the relation of Moses and Aaron, Aaron is the older, the "greater" in age—and therefore, in power. He is to be High Priest, literally, the *Great* Priest. But Moses' compliance becomes an enigmatic form of greatness.

And yet, Moses' sense of injury is justified. He had some right to expect that the High Priestly role would be his. Perhaps in light of the paradigms of Genesis, the notion of primogeniture overturned has become a new convention: the younger brother proves himself to be the child of destiny and supersedes the older, the "greater." Abel, Isaac, Jacob, and Joseph are the most prominent examples. Moreover, as the recipient of all God's instruction about the Tabernacle, Moses is justified in expecting to become the prime actor within its precincts. The shock of exclusion, therefore, represents a reversion to the original typology, to the domination of the elder brother.

Another midrash refines and sharpens the point. At Moses' first encounter with God at the Burning Bush, God had addressed him: "Moses! Moses! . . . Do not come closer . . ." (Ex. 3:4–5):

> And he replied, "Here I am!" . . . "Here I am, ready for priesthood and for kingship! . . ." God replied, "Do not approach closer—that is, your children will not offer sacrifices (lit., bring close to Me), because the priesthood is reserved for Aaron your brother . . . and the kingship for King David." And yet Moses attained both: the priesthood, when he officiated during the seven days of Inauguration of the Tabernacle, and the kingship, as it is written, "Then he became King in Jeshurun" (Deut. 33:5).[11]

The ground on which the midrashic theme is based is the phrase, *Al tikrav halom*—"Do not come closer." This kind of intimacy, the offering of sacrifices—*hakrava*, bringing close— is not your prerogative. "*Your children* will not offer sacrifices": it is the hereditary nature of the priesthood that disqualifies

Moses—just as the first wife's infertility is the reason for the second marriage. Moses loses the priesthood—although he himself does perform the role during the Inauguration of the Tabernacle—because he lacks some reproductive capacity. (It is striking that Moses' biological children are not his spiritual heirs. They play no role in the history of the Exodus or in the wilderness.)

Moses cannot "propagate" his connection to God; he cannot reproduce himself. Like the wife in the midrash, he is "close" to God, he has a natural affinity with the divine, but this kind of affinity does not lend itself to replication.[12] Moses' encounter with the divine is perhaps by its very nature inimitable. Mystical sources read the expression, "man of God" (Deut. 33:1), as referring to an intimate erotic relation that transcends transmission or propagation.

Moses' "infertility" becomes the ground for denying him the High Priesthood. But why is Moses surprised when God tells him to "bring Aaron close" into this dynastic role? If he knows from his encounter with God at the Burning Bush that, despite his "readiness," he will be disqualified for the priesthood, how can he be disappointed when the moment of inauguration arrives? A disappointment that is expected is not exactly a disappointment! But at the later moment, as in the parable of the abandoned wife, a theoretical knowledge becomes shockingly real and immediate. It is as though Moses has "forgotten" God's warning at the Burning Bush. His amnesia is disrupted when God uses the same word *hakrev*—"Bring him close!"—as He had used at the Burning Bush. Earlier, Moses had repressed his experience of loss, and therefore he had not mourned the loss. Now, what he has known from the beginning is reenacted in all its fullness.

In Moses' life, a kind of amnesia makes its appearance more than once. Repeatedly, he seems both to know and not to know of an essential loss. Midrashic versions of Moses' life repeatedly bring to light this dynamic of forgetting and re-membering. Toward the end of the forty-year journey in the wilderness, for instance, God abruptly decrees that Moses will not consummate his journey by leading his people into the Land. This tragic declaration is made in mysterious circum-stances, after Moses has struck the rock at Meriva to produce water for his people: "Because you have not trusted Me to sanctify Me before the eyes of the children of Israel, therefore you shall not bring this community into the land which I have given them" (Num. 20:12). Clearly, this is a shocking moment for Moses and Aaron. And yet, according to midrashic sources, Moses had been told from the beginning of the story that he would not lead the people to their destination.[13] Again, the same dynamic: the present crisis catalyzes an old, suspended knowl-edge of loss.

A repressed memory is rearranged, rewritten under the vital impact of present knowledge. Freud named this dynamic *Nachträglichkeit*. Perhaps all these obscured traumas of Moses' life gesture toward a primal loss that has never been fully ac-knowledged? In psychoanalytic terms, it is the loss of the mother that forms the primal stratum, forgotten and re-transcribed, of experience. The loss of the mother, quite literally in Moses' case, engenders in him a continual quest for echoes of that loss.

The Crown of Torah

In the midrash about the compliant wife, God consoles Moses for the loss of the High Priesthood. He names his com-pensation *Torah*, which saves the world from extinction: "I had possession of the Torah, and I gave it to you: if it were not for the Torah I should have lost My world!" In other words, Moses, who lacks the reproductive capacity that biologically preserves the human race, is endowed with another world-preserving ca-pacity. Playing on a verse from Psalms ("If Your Torah had not been my play, I should have perished in my poverty" [Ps. 119:92]), God tells Moses: "If it were not for the Torah, which I have given you, *I* should have lost *My* world!"

The divine world is the world of *play with Torah texts.* Moses becomes the prototype of those who engage in this divine play, separating words and letters and connecting them in different formations. His role is of incomparable significance. It involves losses, gestures of compliance that are read as gestures of spontaneous greatness. Generic rather than genetic, Moses' role is seen in later texts as representing the ongoing generativity that preserves God's world.

Moses' place in this world is nevertheless enigmatic. At the moment when he is told to yield place to his brother, the Torah has God address him with the emphatic pronoun *Ve-atta:* "*As for you,* bring close your brother . . ." This emphatic address is repeated several times in the immediate context—three times within five verses (Ex. 27:20; 28:1, 3) We would normally expect *Ve-atta* to set up a contrast with another subject. Here, since Moses is the subject of the entire passage, it is not clear why the text targets him at this point.

Ironically, too, the Torah portion in which the triple address occurs is the only one in which Moses' name is entirely absent. A tension forms between absence and emphatic presence: a moment of loss and gain. Just where Moses is asked to comply in yielding his brother the dignities of a dynastic role, God insists on the intimate invocation: "Now you . . . you . . . you."[14]

A quiet pulse sounds within the text that celebrates Aaron's official inauguration. God has apparently shifted the center of gravity away from Moses to Aaron. Moses is left with a merely instrumental role. But the pulse of *Ve-atta* evokes a new kind of power. The balance of forces is subtly re-centered. Losses and gains shift their meanings.

Moses is asked to accept—like the compliant wife—a place

of distance and loneliness, in which he will re-create union in the mode of play. Surrendering the priestly garments, which speak the language of representation—public, ceremonious, relatively static—Moses is to create a *playful* language—in fact, a poetic language. "If Your Torah had not been my play (*sha'ashua*), I should have perished in my poverty."

This *sha'ashua*, this playfulness, is entirely serious work: God's world depends on it. The poet plays in the space that John Keats names *negative capability:* "where a man is capable of being in uncertainties, Mysteries, doubts, without any irritable reaching after fact and reason."[15] In this space, one is capable of eluding rigid forms; one moves into and out of many roles. One can even, in Keats's self-description, become a sparrow pecking at the gravel: ". . . if a Sparrow come before my Window, I take part in its existence and pick about the Gravel."[16]

The culture of *sha'ashua* arises precisely when law is crystallized, transmitted in written or engraved form, when the creative surge seems frozen in place. This is a moment of danger, when God's world becomes brittle. In the view of a number of commentators, while the formalism and ceremoniousness of the priesthood is given to Aaron, Moses becomes the agent of that different valence of spirituality that will be called the Oral Torah, the Torah of the Mouth.[17]

Moses becomes the type of those who generate complex, irreducible interpretations, poems in themselves. His special responsibility will be the olive oil for the Menorah, the candelabrum in the Tabernacle. R. Naftali Tzvi Yehuda Berlin of Volozhin (known as the Ha'amek Davar) discusses the "wondrous" symbolic power of the Menorah; its seven branches and its elaborate knobs and blossoms suggest a fantastic beauty of wisdom and ingenuity.[18]

In this view, Moses' genius is quite different from that of Aaron. His is the "crown of Torah," which, unlike the crown of priesthood, or the crown of royalty, is not hereditary. It is, according to Maimonides, potentially accessible to every Jew: "Whoever wishes may come and take of it!" Democratic in essence, its authority transcends and is the source of the authority of the other two crowns. Moses-figures, in every generation, move beyond fixed forms of understanding toward new combinations of words that, Godlike, create worlds.

Who is the Moses who emerges from this portrait of brotherhood? He is the man without fixed identity—in a sense, childless; in a sense, parentless; child of two cultures, Hebrew and Egyptian, and marginal, in a sense, to both. He cannot, at first, find himself in any language. A protean figure, he wears many crowns, but he is absorbed into no single role. Neither priest nor king, he will know both crowns. Momentarily absent from the text, he is yet pervasive. He is the other, who expresses what the structures repress.

His project is the discovery of a voice that is uniquely his, "for the sake of Israel." He is to be God's second-person address. He is to respond to his brother with a magnanimous imagination. "As you live," he says, in another midrash, "even though you have become High Priest, it is *as though* I had become High Priest!"[19] A metaphoric genius allows him to lose the hard casing of selfhood in acts of imaginative power.[20] In all this, Moses is inwardly *in process*. As in most processes, there are points of strain. The midrash allows us to glimpse an intimate narrative of becoming, with its anger and melancholy, as well as its luminous harmonies.

2. MIRIAM

Secret Meanings

There is yet another dramatic confrontation between Moses and Aaron, this time together with their other sibling Miriam. In this mysterious episode, narrated in Numbers 12, Miriam and Aaron speak against Moses—*be-moshe*—protesting his singular claims to prophecy: "Is it only *be-moshe*, through Moses, that God has spoken? Has He not spoken through us too?" (Num. 12:1–2). Moses becomes an object of envy within his own family. Miriam, who is the moving spirit of this conflict, is afflicted with leprosy and isolated from the camp, until the seven-day quarantine period is over.

The central issue of the narrative is Moses' difference from all other prophets, including his own siblings. To Miriam, particularly, this difference looks like arrogance: God has spoken *through* her and *through* Aaron in the same way as *through Moses*. God's answer is trenchant: *Lo chen*—"*Not so*—*not like others*—is My servant Moses!" (12:7). Moses is a world of his own, fundamentally different from all other prophets. It is not arrogance but, strangely, humility that characterizes him in his difference (12:3).

Difference and sameness: within his own family, Moses lives in the eye of that storm. In Miriam, particularly, midrashic sources trace currents of feeling that run deep: they detect a sexual motif in her protest. Drawing on the mysterious reference to a "Cushite woman whom he had married" (12:1), Rashi tells a story of a separation, rather than a marriage: Moses had *separated* from his wife Tzippora (here called the Cushite woman), abstaining from sexual relations because of the demands of his prophetic condition.[21] In this reading, Miriam's envy is complicated by her conviction that there need be no tension between sexuality and prophetic experience. She and Aaron have received prophecy without interrupting their sexual lives. Miriam comes to know about Moses' private life and sharply protests against his celibate state.

In the midrashic narratives, as recounted by Rashi, secret meanings subvert the apparent narrative. Miriam is aggrieved not at Moses' marriage, but at his separation from his own wife. I suggest that when she protests against his splitting between sexual and prophetic experience, she draws on the origins of her relationship with him. We remember that when she first appears in the biblical narrative, she is holding vigil over her baby brother, who floats in a box, a basket, on the Egyptian river. In the event, she restores the infant Moses to his own mother's breast, until he is weaned. Miriam is a maternal surrogate, enabling the physical reunion of mother and child. Why, in this moment of danger, does she play the maternal role?

Midrashic traditions fill in a backstory. Miriam's special connection with Moses begins before his birth. At the height of the Egyptian genocide, when baby boys were to be thrown into the river, Miriam's father separated from his wife. Miriam then confronted her father with her conviction that he is doing Pharaoh's work: "Your decree is harsher than Pharaoh's: he decreed against male children, while your decree prevents any child from being born!"[22] In response to her protest, her parents reunite and Moses is born.

This midrashic narrative positions Miriam as the daughter who makes possible the birth of her younger brother. She is, in a sense, a co-mother; her critique of sexual separation brings Moses into the world. Her relation with her younger brother is, therefore, unusually intense and complex. And years later, when that brother separates from his wife, her passion for connection is again aroused.

The moment of confrontation with her father, the man of "decrees," is recorded in the midrash as her moment of prophecy.[23] But this moment is unrecorded in the biblical text; it is celebrated cryptically, years later, at the Red Sea, when she is given the title "Miriam the prophetess, Aaron's sister" (Ex. 15:20). "When did she prophesy?" asks Rashi. "When she was *Aaron's sister*, before Moses was born!" She prophesied the birth of Moses who would redeem the Israelites from Egypt; and then, in the lonely force of her prophetic vision, she stood guard over his basket in the river. Standing "at a distance," she is alienated from her own family, who now doubt her prophecy.[24] Shamed, excluded, her prophecy in question, she bears it staunchly within her like a pregnancy, waiting to know its outcome.

In this powerful midrashic narrative, Miriam is the type of the courageous but despised prophet. This is the moment when she moves from being "Aaron's sister" to being most truly *Moses'* sister (2:4). This moment is deeply implanted within her. It will emerge later in two different forms. When she leads the women in song and dance at the sea, the text refers to her as Miriam *the prophetess;* and when she speaks *against* Moses, God declares judgment on her, shaming her: "If her father spat in her face, would she not bear her shame for seven days? Let her be shut out of the camp for seven days, and then let her be readmitted" (Num. 12:15). Strangely, her early history of prophecy is reenacted when God quarantines her; again, her Father puts her at a distance. The Talmud notices another link between the two episodes: "As she waited for Moses [in his basket in the river], so Israel waited for her in the wilderness."[25]

Alienation and solitude, a father who shames her, a people that gathers her in—at the heart of Miriam's drama is her fraught relation with her brother Moses, which continues throughout her life. Her prophetic role in bringing him into the world endangers her position in her family; as Moses' sister, she risks her identity as her father's daughter. Then, her little brother grows bigger and eclipses her. Her prophecy ceases; his begins and flourishes.

But the main characteristic of her relation with Moses is suggested by the ambiguous preposition *be*—"against" and "through"—that throbs through the later story of envy. Miriam and Aaron *speak against* Moses; and they protest, "Is it only *through* Moses (*be-moshe*) that God has *spoken?* Has He not also *spoken through* us (*banu*)!" The same preposition is used with different meanings: it expresses an adversary relation, a targeted aggressiveness; and it expresses the inward experience of prophecy—God's *speaking in* or *through* a person, in a vision or a dream. When God explains Moses' difference, He uses the same preposition in the same two senses: "Mouth to mouth, I *speak through* him! . . . Why have you not been afraid to *speak against* My servant, *against* Moses?" (12:8). The text then sums up this section of the narrative: "God's anger burned *against* them."

What emerges from this use of the preposition is the intensity of a relationship that is both hostile and deeply empathic. Projection and envy are the shorthand terms for this complexity. Miriam knows what it is to have God speak through her, and she desires to be again a vessel for divine inspiration. In her fantasy, she is merged with Moses, the brother she has "mothered" into the world. It is inconceivable that her vision, in which the sexual and the spiritual are fused, should be different from that of Moses. She speaks, therefore, in and through his imagined world, and against the sexual separation by which Moses expresses his singularity. What bond could be deeper than the bond between this sister-mother and this brother-child? But for him separation from his wife is God's will, and God acknowledges his intuition. His relation with God is unique and all-consuming—*peh el peh*, mouth to mouth.

God too speaks in the language of double meanings, picking up the ambiguity of Miriam's use of *be-*, even as His anger burns against—and within—her. Aaron, praying for his sister, touches off similar depths as he speaks of the shared, half-consumed flesh of siblings: "Let her not be as one dead, who emerges from his mother's womb with half his flesh eaten away!" (Num. 12:12). If Moses' sister, who has come forth from the womb of his mother, is afflicted with leprosy, then it is as though half his flesh, too, is consumed.

The macabre image conveys Aaron's understanding of the intimate connection between Miriam and Moses. All three siblings emerged from the same womb—and siblings are one flesh.[26] But Aaron speaks of *his* (Moses') mother's womb, and of *his* flesh alone. Moses has the power to intercede for his sister, precisely because of the primal connection between them. They emerged from their mother's womb in a unique sense: for Miriam, by reuniting her parents, had brought that womb back into the world of possibilities.

The primal connection created by the flesh and the imagination of those who emerge from the same womb is expressed in unusually charged language. Aaron is here entering into the private world of meanings that is shared by Miriam and Moses. And Moses responds with the briefest, convulsive prayer— "God, please, heal her please!"—from his own flesh, a cry stronger than empathy.

Singularity and Solidarity

Moses' position in this story is harder to detect than that of his passionate sister. Throughout the episode, except for his prayer, Moses is silent. It is God who "hears" the implications of Miriam and Aaron's complaint. At this point, Moses is described: "the man Moses was very humble, more than any other human being on the face of the earth" (12:3). God then speaks about Moses' singularity. How are we to imagine Moses' personal reaction to the family drama of love and envy in which he is involved? Is he impervious to the question of his difference? Do his siblings' grievances affect him?

The question touches on the issue of brotherhood, in the most personal way. Every time God uses the expression, "your brother Aaron," it holds emotional meaning for the man who had two mothers and two mother tongues, the Egyptian prince whose brothers are slaves. When God describes the forthcoming original encounter of the brothers, He declares, "Here is Aaron your brother the Levite—I know that he is a ready speaker. Even now, he is setting out to meet you, and when he sees you he will rejoice in his heart" (Ex. 4:14). This relation, in its complementarity, is to embody and transcend the tension of brotherhood. But when his brother and sister attack him for not being identical with them, his separateness is reaffirmed. At this juncture, what does his silence say?

On the one hand, God, in a sense, speaks for him, when He characterizes him as uniquely *"ne'eman,* faithful, trustworthy, in all My household" (Num. 12:7). The nineteenth-century Hassidic master, Sefat Emet, interprets this difference of Moses: *ne'eman,* he suggests, means stable, unchanging. All other prophets are transfigured by the prophetic experience. They are ecstatic, beyond themselves: "their faces would flame like torches." Moses alone remains constantly attuned to the wavelengths of the divine. "Mouth-to-mouth" expresses an intimacy without ebbs and flows, in which his true nature remains unchanged. His sexuality is sublimated in *devekut,* a passionate but *even* intimacy with God.

This reading imagines Moses' unique way of living as a man who is "the man of God." It speaks of a kind of detachment from the tides of human emotion. But in this incident with his sister, Aaron calls on his solidarity, his brotherly attunement with Miriam. For the first time, Moses confronts his uneasiness with differences and distances, with the need to negotiate the gaps between himself and others. Even with those who are closest to him, in whom he finds the most poignant reminder of the womb that bore them, there arises that uneasiness. With Miriam, his sister-mother, who finds his difference unthinkable, things fall apart.

He prays for her as "half his flesh." But something new emerges in Moses in this crisis. Being the same and not the same as his sister becomes for Moses a clue to the mystery of brotherhood. Imagining himself as the one who is envied, he is brought up against his own singularity, as well as his womb-identity with his siblings.

A short time before this, Moses had cried to God about the

paradox of his own identity: "Did I conceive this people, did I give birth to it, that You should say to me, Carry it in your bosom, as the wet nurse carries the suckling child—to the land that You swore to its fathers?" (Num. 11:11–12). Using imagery that expresses an inexpressible frustration, he imagines himself as mother to his people, to his brothers. There is a violence in his cry: How can he carry this people in his bosom, as though he had been impregnated with them, had given birth to them, had become their male wet nurse? The demand made on him by God is ultimately a demand that he *speak* to them; and he is as unequipped for that role, as a man is unequipped to conceive, give birth, and suckle. To speak to them, he imagines, would mean to *hold* them, to be entirely present to their needs, to be penetrated by them, even, like Miriam, to give birth to them.

Unlike a mother, or a wife, he is not flesh of their flesh. And yet his imagination dwells on feminine images of nurturance, of deepest connection, of *trustworthiness* in relation to the people. To be an *omen*, a male wet nurse, would be to display in his relation to them the same unchanging stability, the same availability, as God celebrates in the related term *ne'eman*. The demand is that he be constantly attuned to the wavelengths of his people as he is to those of his God. The *devekut*, the passionate intimacy of motherhood, (ideally) without ebbs and flows, is imaginatively present to him. Womb and breasts are implicitly grafted on, as the man Moses imagines the totally unacceptable. In some way, God seems to demand a feminization of his masculine self.

His cry is an utterance that refers to a performative possibility. If he had said, "I conceived this people, I gave birth to it . . . ," this would have met the conditions that the British philosopher J. L. Austin applies to a performative utterance: "to utter the sentence is not to *describe* my doing [a thing] . . . or to state that I am doing it: it is to do it."[27] Examples of the performative utterance include, "I promise," "I bet," "I bequeath," "You are sanctified to me." Moses, on the other hand, *undoes* a possible world at the same time that he alludes to it. His cry is, in a sense, more potent than an explicit performative utterance. It evokes the pathos of uncertainty about what he might become capable of. It perpetuates the prestige of pregnancy, birth, and suckling, while creating a penumbra of different ways of imagining it.

Moses' outburst, which ends in a death wish (11:15), gives voice to ambiguities of sameness and otherness that at first trouble him like a loss of personal power. It echoes within his prayer for his sister who is *half his flesh*. And it bears unexpected fruit in his violent encounter with another member of his family, his cousin Korach.

3. KORACH

A Freudian slip

Korach and Moses confront one another with overt hostility. A political rebellion is afoot; power issues are at stake. Korach defies the leadership of Moses and Aaron: "You have gone too far! For all the community are holy, all of them, and God is in their midst. Why then do you raise yourselves above God's congregation?" (Num. 16:3). The rebels' claim sounds appealingly democratic. Moses "falls on his face" on hearing it.

However, beneath the political surface of the narrative a different confrontation is taking place. Korach and Moses are first cousins, mirror images, each inviting the other to greater self-knowledge. In this sense, they are like the sibling couples we have discussed: Moses and Aaron, Moses and Miriam. Here, too, the issue is the tension around sameness and difference. Korach speaks a rhetoric of totality: "*All* the community are holy, *all* of them . . ." Oceanic holiness is the condition of the people, without nuance or conflict or difference. This claim contains enough truth to be persuasive: the camp of Israel is *potentially* holy, and its symbolic center is the Tabernacle with God inhabiting its recesses. But the totality of the rhetoric signals demagoguery. Such a language leaves Moses *speechless*—prostrate, mouth in the earth.

A famous midrash heightens the drama by suggesting that all the rebels deck themselves out in *tallitot she-kulan techelet*, prayer-shawls that are entirely made of blue thread. In place of the single blue thread that is commanded and that signifies a slender link with the transcendent (sea, sky, the throne of glory),[28] they stand flaunting a total holiness—heavenly blue as far as the eye can see—and taunt Moses: "Do *these* garments still require a thread of blue?" Their sarcasm is clear: in the face of the oceanic holiness of the people, how can you insist on the *difference* of a particular man, or a particular family, or symbolic object? The image speaks louder than a thousand words in ridiculing and silencing Moses. What can be said in reply to the theatrics of totality? The rebels have, effectively, put an end to language.

Moses falls on his face; he is struck dumb. Or, as Rashi puts it, "Moses' hands fall limp." His sense of personal power ebbs in a collapse of face and limbs; but surprisingly, he swiftly recovers and begins to speak. He speaks at length, first to Korach and his group, then to Korach alone, and, finally, to the other rebel leaders, Dathan and Aviram. Transcending his despair, he attempts to engage the rebel leaders in dialogue.

But Korach has no reply; Moses' words fall on deaf ears:

> With all these arguments, Moses tried to win Korach over, yet you do not find that the latter returned him any answer. This was because he was clever in his wickedness and thought: If I answer him, I know quite well that he is a very wise man and will presently overwhelm me with his arguments, so that I shall be reconciled to him against my will. It

is better that I should not engage with him. When Moses saw that there was no good to be got of him he took leave of him . . .

"And Moses sent to call Dathan and Aviram" (v. 12). They too persisted in their wickedness and did not deign to answer him. "And they said: We will not come up. These wicked people were tripped up by their own mouth; there is a covenant made with the lips—for they died and *went down* into the bottomless abyss, after they had "*gone down* alive into the underworld" (v. 33). "And Moses was very angry" (v. 15). Why? Because when a man argues with his companion and the other answers him in argument, he has satisfaction, but if he does not answer he feels aggrieved.[29]

In the view of the midrash, Moses attempts to make peace with Korach, who is too canny to respond. Korach considers Moses' power with words to be dangerous, seductive. Perhaps it is language itself that he senses as treacherous.

Compelled to abandon this project, Moses turns to the other rebels, where he fares just as poorly. Dathan and Aviram do in fact technically reply to Moses' overture, but the gist of their reply is *Lo na'aleh—We will not come up!* In other words, they use words to refuse dialogue, beginning and ending their scathing speech by repeating *Lo na'aleh!* Their reply is a verbal sneer.

Here, our midrash makes a startling interpretation: "They were tripped up by their own mouth; there is a covenant made with the lips." Dathan and Aviram find themselves speaking beyond their conscious knowledge. As in what we now call the Freudian slip, their words run away with them: refusing to *come up*, they will very shortly find themselves on the way *down* to the underworld. Unwittingly, they foretell their own macabre fate.

Perhaps they are not so much foretelling as *testifying* to the course they are already set upon. Rejecting language, refusing to treat with Moses, they are already turned toward death. The biblical motif of "the silence of the grave" is implicit here. "The dead shall not praise God, nor any that go down into silence," says the Psalmist.[30] The dead cannot speak, praise, communicate. Silence becomes in many biblical passages a synonym for death. In choosing not to respond to Moses' call, the rebels have refused language; they have chosen death over life. If they will not *come up*, they are already on the way down to the silent shades.

Speech as Trauma

Moses' angry reaction becomes in the midrash a deep *grief*.[31] This is presented as a normal human reaction to being ignored by another. But, we may remember, Moses has a particular reason to be pained by such an experience. In terms of his personal history, when his overtures fall on deaf ears, his worst fears are fulfilled. At the Burning Bush, at the very beginning of his mission, he had shied away from God's call with the words: "But they will not believe me, they *will not listen to my voice*, they will say: God never appeared to you!" (Ex. 4:1). Pleading his inability to make the people listen to him, he went on to use idioms and metaphors to convey his rejection of God's mission: "Please, O God, I have never been a man of words, neither yesterday nor the day before, nor now that You have spoken to Your servant; I am heavy of speech and heavy of tongue" (4:10). "Moses spoke to God, saying, 'The Israelites would not listen to me; how then should Pharaoh listen to me, a man of uncircumcised lips!'" (6:12).

When he complains of being unable to speak, he means he is unable to make people listen to him. If the other refuses to respond, clearly communication has failed. To *speak* in the fullest sense is to make the other speak, to elicit a response.[32] It is this nexus of communication that from the outset arouses dread in Moses. Now, in his scene with the rebels, it seems that his dread is realized in the most painful way. Reaching out to them, his gesture meeting with no response, an old wound reopens: he has failed to *speak*.

God responds in an unexpected way to Moses' complaint at the Burning Bush. Instead of reassuring him, promising him communicative power, God asks a question: "What is that in your hand?" This is the scene that follows:

> And he replied, "A rod." He said, "Cast it on the ground." He cast it on the ground and it became a snake; and Moses fled from it. Then God said to Moses, "Put out your hand and grasp it by the tail"—he put out his hand and seized it, and it became a rod in his hand—"so that they may believe that God, the God of their father, the god of Abraham, the God of Isaac, and the God of Jacob, did appear to you."
>
> God said to him further, "Put your hand into your bosom." He put his hand into his bosom; and when he took it out, his hand was encrusted with snowy scales! And He said, "Put your hand back into your bosom."—He put his hand back into his bosom; and when he took it out of his bosom, there it was again like his own flesh. (4:2–7)

Instead of healing Moses of his oral dread, God enacts with him the very experience, in the flesh, of his dread. The rod in his hand is no sooner named as such than it becomes a snake— "And Moses fled from it." An object that has just emerged from his own body, a safe, definable object, which was, in a sense, a symbolic extension of the power of his hand, now arouses in him an uncontrollable, visceral fear. In an instant, as it leaves his hand, it becomes unrecognizable, terrifying. Then, at God's command, he overcomes his fear and grasps the snake, which re-transforms in his hand into a rod. "This is the first sign," designed to create belief in the Israelites (4:8); but a sign, as well, to himself, a staging of his own fear of that which emerges from his body and can no longer be mastered.

The second sign is even closer to the bone: his hand emerges from his bosom covered with snowy scales; when he puts it back in his bosom and again withdraws it, it has been restored *kivsaro*—to be part of his flesh again. Here, Moses' very flesh goes dead as it goes forth toward the world—a kind of ghastly birth. The very same movement of *in-out* then brings his hand back to life, to become again his own flesh.

I suggest that these signs, in addition to their public role—to convince the people of the truth of Moses' claim that God indeed appeared to him—have another purpose: Moses is being brought face to face with the dynamic of his own fear. Both signs reenact the trauma of the act of speech: the movement from an interior to an exterior world, and the dread of what cannot be controlled in that communication. In speaking, in meeting the other, there is sacrifice, there is transformation, even a fantasy of losing oneself. Taken through a flesh-parable of fear, death, and resurrection, Moses must think of the edges of his body, his hand, his skin—and of that quintessential edge which is the mouth.[33] Here, the self touches the outer world; here, volatile changes and exchanges take place. This is the site of desire and fear, the boundary that creates longing and recoil. Between the lips rises the erotic space, the wish to transmit messages, to dissolve boundaries.

A Zone of Vulnerability

This erotic reach gives life to language, flouting the edges of things, enhancing meaning, inspired by an impossible desire. It begins with the first oral experience of the infant at the mother's breast.

As we have seen, the Torah devotes considerable space to a description of Moses' infant nursing history. Clearly, if the baby Moses is to be saved from the fate of Israelite male infants, some provision will have to be made for feeding him. But the fact that the Torah gives prominence to this technical issue (the wet nurse is a common resource in ancient aristocracies) signals a site of tension.

Miriam, Moses' sister, volunteers to bring Moses' mother to act as a surrogate for the Egyptian princess. But several verses (Ex. 2:7–10) then recount, in slow motion, how his mother is hired and how she feeds her own child, as though to allow the reader to dwell on the paradox of the situation. Moses is to be nurtured by the princess's hired surrogate—who happens to be his birth mother.

Rashi quotes from the Talmud: "The princess tried out many Egyptian wet nurses, but he refused to nurse, because he was destined to speak with the Shechina" (B. Sotah 12b). Here, the double sense of orality is explicit: the mouth that will speak with God cannot feed from impure breasts. The basic oral impulse—to feed—is in this child inhibited at the earliest stage. Fraught with his future, precociously dedicated to an ultimate conversation, he cannot inhabit his body, reach beyond its edges with full spontaneity. Even when he is reunited with his mother, she nurses him in a double role—as his mother and as the princess's surrogate.[34] Radiations from the future inhibit both tactility and language.

We have noticed the possible connection between this experience of alienation and his later description of his relation to his people: "Did I conceive this entire people, did I bear them, that You should say to me, 'Carry them in your bosom as a wet nurse carries an infant,' to the land that You have promised on oath to their fathers?" (Num. 11:12). The bizarre image of Moses as failed male wet nurse suggests a deep frustration, a yearning for a simpler, more organic world of connection. Wishing and fearing to feed, to be fed, to speak, to evoke response, Moses knows the traumatic gap that makes *dibbur*, the human speech function, a zone of vulnerability.

The World of *As-If*

Returning now to the Korach narrative, we may appreciate the history of Moses' despair. When the rebels make their stand, with their dazzling and unanswerable assertion of total holiness, "Moses heard, and he fell on his face" (16:4). After this moment of speechlessness, he attempts to speak to Korach and to Dathan and Aviram. Both overtures are rejected, one in silence and the other in words of repudiation. But the fact that he tries again after Korach has rebuffed him becomes the trigger for an important Talmudic teaching: "From here we learn that one should not persist in a *machloket*, in a dispute, for Moses sought them out [lit., courted them] in order to come to terms with them through a peaceful dialogue."[35]

The imagery of courtship, with its erotic implication, evokes a Moses who is willing to sacrifice his dignity in his desire for connection with the rebels. A tension is set up between the static hold of *machloket* and the dynamic, even seductive project of speech. To persist (lit., hold on tight) in *machloket* is to create a rigid, unchangeable situation. Moses overcomes the compulsive hold of *machloket;* in terms of his personal history, he overcomes his own impulse to retire into silence. He reaches out beyond his edges to "court" Korach, and then Dathan and Aviram.

The sarcastic reply of the latter raises further questions about language:

> And they said, "We will not come up! Is it not enough that you brought us out from a land flowing with milk and honey to have us die in the wilderness, that you would also lord it over us? You have not even brought us a land flowing with milk and honey, and given us possession of fields and vineyards—Will you gouge out these men's eyes? We will not come up!" (Num. 16:12–14)

Beginning and ending their speech with refusal, Dathan and Aviram repeat, "We will not come up!"[36] As we have noticed, the midrash reads this as referring ominously to their final descent into the earth. We suggested that this descent reflects the movement away from language, downward into silence.

In addition, on a conscious level, the rebels mock Moses' pretensions: he claims to be bringing them up, to life and to the inheritance of the Land, when the reality is that they will all die in the wilderness. *Lo na'aleh* implies, then, "Your use of idioms of *aliya* (ascending) is mere propaganda. The truth behind your rhetoric is *yerida*, loss, the final descent to death."[37] The rebels caustically remind Moses that the whole generation is condemned to die in the wilderness; there is no meaning to Moses' description of a future *aliya:* "We will not be ascending into the promised future." In sophisticated fashion, they expose the fictions of his language.

Seforno makes an even more sophisticated suggestion. The rebels say, "You have not even . . . given us possession of fields" (16:14). However, in Hebrew, this reads as a positive statement (lit., "you *have given* us . . ."). The word *not* must be carried forward from the previous phrase. However, Seforno reads: "Is it not enough that you have brought us out of a land flowing with milk and honey to this wilderness, but *you are also mocking us: your rhetoric pretends* that you are giving us an inheritance of fields and vineyards. Every time you speak about the commandments to be fulfilled in the Land, it is *as though* the Land is really to be ours, with its fields and vineyards."

In this reading, the rebels are exposing the propaganda language of a ruler who is trying to pull the wool over their eyes—in the text, to gouge out their eyes. Unmasking his rhetoric, the rebels accuse Moses of demagoguery. More than that, they express a deep distrust of language itself. Twice, Seforno uses the word *k'eelu* ("as if") about Moses' way of using language. "You are mocking us, playing with us," they claim. But perhaps what they cannot tolerate is the very nature of language—playful, metaphorical to the core. *Your words are "as if,"* they say. Perhaps all significant language is *as if,* referring only partly to a demonstrable reality.

Their disenchanted sneer is itself unmasked. The world of *dibbur,* of language, is a world of *as if,* which acknowledges imagination, desire, the role of *eros.* The fiction of the future, the ongoing invention of the self, the attempt to dissolve boundaries—these are all part of the project of language. As Jacques Lacan puts it, *Les non-dupes errent*—"Those who will not be duped are themselves in error."[38] Compulsively suspicious, the rebels attack Moses' language, ignoring their own implication in the world of *dibbur.* They may, in fact, be the most duped of all, since their own fantasy world remains unacknowledged.

In his struggle for integrity in language, Moses is now faced with the silence of Korach, on the one hand, and with the verbal sneer of Dathan and Aviram, on the other. Both represent a radical rejection of the world of *dibbur.* Indeed, the drama of this confrontation rises partly from Moses' own history of refusal to speak. But Moses' history indicates a struggle with that refusal. From the moment when he describes himself as "of uncircumcised lips," there is born in him an awareness of an *impediment,* a block to be overcome.[39]

Uncannily, Moses sees a version of himself in his cousin Korach. Both men, in different ways, are possessed by a suspicion of language. But for the first time Moses hears of his own unknown power with words. Strangely, Korach expresses his fear of that power, so that Moses is compelled to adjust his own sense of incapacity. At the same time, he witnesses as in a distorted mirror the effects of the refusal to speak. Korach's silence tells of his withdrawal from the life-drama of language, and Dathan and Aviram's suspicion of metaphor mirrors Moses' own fastidiousness. Even as they mock him, they perform their own deathward fall into silence.

Eros and Language

In a provocative discussion of Korach's "disputatious" stance,[40] Maharal diagnoses Korach's personality as destructively self-righteous. Speaking from a place of total rightness, of *din*, such people bring ruin upon the world. Korach avoids debate; he is so "right" that he can make no space for discussion. As "master of dissension," he suffers from a kind of manic rationality. His words avoid metaphor, real questions, any indication of the human incompleteness that inspires language. In this sense, he represents a *resistance* to language.

Ironically, in this reading, the *machloket* (disputatious) mentality avoids debate, argument, the exchange that affects both sides. Maharal's narrative brings to mind G. K. Chesterton's provocative statement: "The madman is not the man who has lost his reason. The madman is the man who has lost everything except his reason. . . . His mind moves in a perfect but narrow circle."[41] The perfect circle of the mad mind may take the form of a world of wholly holy people, undifferentiated from one another and from themselves, defined by their rightness.

In a different language, a classic narrative of creation tells of how the Infinite One, who encompasses all reality, retracted His light, so as to leave space—a *challal panui*—in which, through language, to project a world as ours, with boundaries, separations, objects, space, and time. This act of divine self-limitation is known as *tzimtzum*.

R. Nahman of Bratzlav, the nineteenth-century Hassidic master, reshapes this cosmological model, first developed in the kabbalistic teachings of R. Isaac Luria, in order to speak of the creation of cultural worlds, worlds of human meaning.

This creation, too, depends on the gap of incompleteness, where the discourse of scholars, for instance, can leave space *between* them for new worlds of thought to form. Between any two who speak or argue, it is the void allowed by each, the willingness to suspend prejudices, that opens to unpredictable insight.

The philosopher Walter Benjamin writes: "Friendship does not abolish the distance between human beings, but brings that distance to life."[42] This, too, for R. Nahman, is the role of *machloket:* to bring to life worlds not yet seen. This gestation requires a space—the irreducible distance between human beings.

Korach, averse to spaces, suspicious of speech, is declared in the Zohar to have "repudiated the creation of the world." This mystifying statement is profoundly connected with the Lurianic concept of *tzimtzum*. Korach is allergic to voids, breaches in the perfect circle of rationality, to the erotic reach of language itself. Intelligent, sane, like Chesterton's madman, he is incapable of the movement of desire.

In this analysis, Korach's resistance arises out of a profound disorientation in the world. And Moses very well understands his allergic response to language. For Moses, however, a struggle has long been under way to revive the maternal tongue. As we have suggested, this would mean, in Julia Kristeva's terms, acknowledging the loss of the mother and mourning her loss. To recover language from the repressed state she calls asymbolia, one needs to *lose*, to experience a void, a break, a renunciation. Sometimes, this is approached precisely by *negating* the repressed idea (the loss of the mother). Citing Freud, she sees in negation a freeing of the mind that can now partially accept the unacceptable idea. Here the symbolic process may begin, in an acknowledgment through denial.

Perhaps we can hear Moses' protestations in this way: "I am not a man of words . . . I am heavy of mouth and heavy of tongue . . . of uncircumcised lips . . ." Perhaps even, "Did I conceive this people, did I give birth to them, that You say to me,

Carry them in your bosom, as a wet nurse carries the suckling infant?" Rhetorical questions function as negations, which, in their own way, acknowledge loss. For Moses, a recovery of language would mean a recovery of desire. As part of that process, Moses sees his cousin Korach as mirroring his own struggles with language.

Voids and Differences

But against this background of sameness, Moses' difference from Korach emerges in high relief. When, for instance, Moses falls on his face, he enacts his speechlessness in the face of a world that he knows well, a world that makes speech redundant (a sea of blue, with no void for desire). But when Moses begins to speak and to "court" the rebels he sets a distance between himself and his cousin, as well as, perhaps, a distance from his former self—a distance to be bridged by language. With gaps and voids comes the erotic reach toward the other.

Mei HaShiloah, the modern Hassidic master, diagnoses Korach's malaise in terms that are quite similar to the ones we have explored.[43] Korach, he says, has no access to his own void, his *chissaron*, his incompleteness. Most pitiable of human beings, he is "lost"—a reference to the description of Korach's disappearance into the earth. Some essential dimension of humanity is blocked from his view. This has to do with differences, with gaps between people and with a similar blindness to his own internal gaps, places of difference from his own conscious self. These inner blind spots make growth impossible.

To be redeemed, Korach would need to discover a critical new awareness of his *chissaron*, his human shortcomings—and of the difference *between himself and Moses*. By putting it in these terms, Mei HaShiloah is suggesting that the nub of the story is precisely this question of difference. He imagines a possible reversal for Korach's locked-in state. In a sense, there must be such a possibility—a human being must be capable of moments of revelation; otherwise, the perfect, narrow circle of madness will prevail: an unthinkable prospect. The reversal must come in a moment of uncanny insight: Korach and Moses are different, one aware of his *chissaron*, the other not. At least insofar as Korach might acknowledge this difference, he might gain access to his own internal void and—like Moses—begin to speak.

What Moses comes in this narrative to represent, then, is the movement toward language. Acknowledging himself as *aral sefatayim*—"of uncircumcised lips/edges" (Ex. 6:12)—he recognizes the "foreskin," the impediment, that needs to be removed. Now, a project is born: the opening of his body and mind to a sense of its own incompleteness—a circumcision of sorts.

With this movement comes a sense of his difference *from himself.* No longer all of a piece with himself or with the world, aware of his edges, internal and external, Moses is reborn as a *speaking* being, capable of symbolic thinking and therefore of creating his own specific world. A fantasy of wholeness is relinquished. The philosopher Jacques Maritain speaks of "some abiding despair in every great poet, a certain wound in him that has set free the creativeness."[44] The awareness of a wound, an "abiding despair," brings Moses too to a new voice.

Such a history of Moses reaches us by way of indirection. In a sense, imagining Moses as a great poet may seem a literary luxury. In the traditional view, everything important that Moses said was a transmission of God's words, so that we might say that his own creativity, his own poetic voice, is neither here nor there. However, at least in the many moments when he is speaking in his own voice—to God, to his people, to the Egyptians, and to himself—there is clearly a self, a subjectivity at work, which is, with all its difference, a recognizably human subjectivity. Moses' prophetic greatness has everything to do with the singular force of his language. Most importantly, there is a dynamic, a *movement* of sensibility at work, reflexive, aware of its own *chissaron*—of the wound at the root of his being.

The great French-Jewish philosopher Emmanuel Levinas calls this *chissaron* the "fracture" that opens one up to revelation. This fracture breaks one open and allows the shock of otherness—the relationship with the face of the other, which is the immediate arena of revelation. When one welcomes one's neighbor, when one greets him with *hineni* ("Here I am"), one exposes oneself to a divine *worry*—the "uncontainable impact of God's Infinity"—which is divine inspiration.[45] Because of this fracture, one's own I is called into question: "The voice coming from another shore teaches transcendence itself."[46] Prejudices, rigidities, easy assumptions about the other are suspended in such "face-to-face" moments.

Moses is the key figure in such a theology. His stammer gives him access to a relation with an Other that is "better than self-possession."[47] "The language of the Old Testament is so suspicious of any rhetoric without a stammer that it has as its chief prophet a man 'slow of speech and of tongue.'"[48] His is to be a language that never forgets its stammer, the difference between inner and outer worlds, between self and other.

"There is a crack in everything"

One last witness to the connection between Moses and Korach is the modern Hassidic master Sefat Emet. He takes us to the beginning of the world—and to the end of the Korach narrative. He too tells of the *chissaron*, the incompleteness from which the world suffers. This is an essential incompleteness, which allows, on occasion, the victory of *hessed* (grace) over *din* (strict justice). We yearn for wholeness, precisely because, like the troubadours' *amour de loin*, it is far from us.

There is a rupture in human experience—a crack in the cup—which generates this yearning; desire builds toward a transcendent source of grace—*hessed*—such as the Sabbath. The inherent turbulence of the world is exposed at the very moment when creation is completed, in the twilight moment before Shabbat. At this moment of greatest tension, "between the suns," the demons of chaos (*mezikin*—destructive angels, as Sefat Emet calls them) are aroused and, with the onset of Shabbat, laid to rest. The world is made whole for the Shabbat moment.[49]

Here, Sefat Emet brings us back to the Korach narrative. In this primal twilight, "the mouth of the earth (*pi ha'aretz*) was created."[50] This is the crack into which Korach and his followers vanish. It represents all the *chissaron*—the fracture in the world—that Korach set himself to deny. Demonic forces take their revenge on him for his manic rationality. He has closed out the dynamic of longing that lives in language. He has lost the sense of the gaps and edges of human experience, and with it the ability to be permeated by infinity. Like a stone, he sinks into silence.

Conclusive Meaning: The Mouth of the Earth

In bearing witness to Korach, Sefat Emet is also implicitly telling us about the different history of Moses. For Moses too, we have suggested, knows about the fantasy world of totality. For him it is perhaps more real than for any other human being. And yet he is moved toward others, toward Israel, toward himself, across the gaps. Increasingly, he comes to know that he was born into the cracked world in order to let light in. Language will be necessary, even a source of blessing, if he can find the stammering voice with which to speak.

The final scene, the showdown between Moses and Korach, is initiated by Moses' speech of warning:

> By this you shall know that it was God who sent me to do all these things; that they were not of my own devising [lit., not from my heart]: if these men die as all men do, if their lot be

the common fate of all mankind, it was not God who sent me. But if God brings about something unheard-of [lit., if God creates a new creation], so that the ground opens its mouth and swallows them up, with all that belongs to them, and they go down alive into Sheol, you shall know that these men have spurned God. (Num. 16:28–30)

More than a warning, this speech is Moses' theological confrontation with the rebels. It is about God and revelation and difference. Mostly, it is about knowledge: the approaching cataclysm will make the truth of their history apparent. And indeed, "The ground under them burst asunder, and the earth opened its mouth and swallowed them up" (16:31–32). The text insists on the grotesque oral imagery of Moses' scenario. That the ground bursts asunder and the rebels go down to the underworld is apparently not sufficient to convey the scene. The earth must become a maw yawning wide, swallowing up its victims. When does this moment of oral horror arrive? With precision, the narrative presents the timing: "Scarcely had he finished speaking all these words . . ." (16:31).

When Moses stops speaking, when he closes his mouth, the earth opens up its mouth and swallows. Speaking and eating— two oral functions—are in tension. As long as Moses speaks, the mouth of the earth remains closed. When it opens, it is not to speak but to consume. The terrible alternative to spoken words is the cataclysm of final and irrefutable revelations. Moses had, as it were, *exhausted* (*k'chaloto . . . et kol ha-devarim*) all the resources of language, so that nothing remained but the brute apocalypse. The limitation of human language, indeed, is that words can never achieve that finality, the *last word*, of the consuming earth. Moses speaks to the very last moment, in order, in a sense, to hold an option open. Orality is at issue here. Moses speaks not only to warn but also to exercise the power of language, to keep worlds in play. When he closes his mouth, the earth opens its mouth to devastating effect.

In this horrifying scene, Moses stands at the very edge of the pit. When it yawns open and closes over the dead, something conclusive has happened. The truth of Moses' story has been manifested. But this is a situation of final resort. With what feelings does Moses—and those like him who inhabit the difficult ground of language at the edge of the pit—view the closure of the story? The scenario seems to be his idea, since there is no mention of a command from God. Perhaps the apocalyptic scene represents his sense of the limits as well as the power of language. Once again, his early anxiety about not being *heard* is vindicated. Language displays its ultimate weakness. He is heard by God but not by the people. In the end, only the blatant theatricality of the earth's mouth can bring the rebellion to an end.

The Paradox of Song

But the rabbinic sages will not allow the matter to rest there. In spite of the conclusive ending of the story, they insist on reopening it. *"Are the Korach conspirators destined to re-ascend from the underworld?"*[51] There are a number of hypothetical answers to the question. But the question itself is significant. Something is not quite closed: the mouth can still ask questions. After all, there is the mysterious statement a few chapters later: "And the children of Korach did not die" (26:11). A full verse is given to the statement, leaving an impression of an unfinished thought.[52] And Korach's children are later recorded as the singers in the Temple: several of the Psalms are attributed to the sons of Korach. But were they not swallowed up in the general cataclysm of "all Korach's people"? (16:32).

One resolution is offered in the Talmud: "A place was reserved for them in the underworld and they sat there and *sang.*"[53] At the last moment, they repent; or, more precisely, they experience *pangs* (*hirhurim*) of penitence—qualms, pangs of *worry*. They crack open, disrupted, their humanity restored. Perhaps Moses' words did not fall on deaf ears after all.

The songs of Korach's sons are there in the Psalms for all to read. Some, particularly Psalm 88, record the very experience of those whose voices survive to register their own redemption. Repentance and song are forces that reopen the most closed of narratives.

Here, we return to Moses, whose own history includes the paradox of song. It is, again, Sefat Emet, who spoke of the crack through which grace may enter, who draws our attention to Moses' song-moment at the Red Sea: *Az yashir moshe*—"Then Moses sang/would sing . . ." (Ex. 15:1).[54] Rashi reads the unusual future-tense narrative form as a moment of intentionality: "Then there came up in his mind the intention to sing a song." He also quotes the midrashic reading: "This is a biblical reference to the revival of the dead!" Sefat Emet comments: what Moses actually sings is that part of his internal song that lends itself to the words of the world. But a residue remains within, the fantasy of praise that cannot pass—*not yet*—the barrier of consciousness. This unconscious life is what the midrash refers to when it says that the text hints at the resurrection of the dead. Then, infinite desires, expressed only in fragmentary ways in this world, will find full expression. This is the intention that comes up in Moses' mind.

Beyond the words of the song that Moses authors, there is the residue of what cannot yet be sung. "Not yet" sustains the intuition of ultimate possibility. Moses' intention of a future song emerges from his specific experience of speechlessness and song. Beyond his relation with his cousin Korach, there are songs that will yet find words: Korach's sons will sing, and Moses' song will redeem death itself.

5

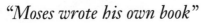

"Moses wrote his own book"

DESIRING THEIR DESIRE

In his final speeches, Moses strikes a new note. As he re-
calls critical episodes of their shared history, a subtle autobiographical thread begins to weave its way through his narrative:

> These are the words that Moses spoke . . . Moses began to
> expound this Torah saying, God our God spoke to us in
> Chorev . . . And I said to you at that time, I can no longer
> bear you alone . . . And I commanded your judges at that
> time . . . And the thing was good in my eyes, and I took
> twelve men from among you . . . (Deut. 1:1–23)

He is the narrator of the saga, and he tells it with quiet emphasis on his own role in it. Most strikingly, he recounts his
own past speeches to the people, in his own words—as he now
remembers them. What comes to light is not only his perspective on the nation's shared history but also his idiosyncratic

memory of his own words, of his own voice echoing through time. This reflexivity gives new voice to Moses' inner world. More precisely, it gives voice to the intersubjective world created between himself and his people. In finding words for his report, he to some extent creates what previously had been only dimly known. As spoken autobiography, his final speeches to his people bring his relation with them into full being.

The Talmud declares that "Moses wrote the book of Job, the story of Balaam, and *his own book*."[1] "His own book" refers to Deuteronomy: it is his own because a large part of it—the final speeches, including his memory of his interactions with his people—is forged in the creative fire of his own mind. Like all creation, Moses' words surprise. Instead of repeating his past speeches, he gives new shape to a complex knowledge whose implications are for the first time revealed.

In this vein, he tells his people of the occasion when he said to them, "I can no longer bear you alone. . . . How can I bear unaided the trouble of you, the burden, and the resentments!" (Deut. 1:9, 12). Moses' complaint had resulted in the formation of a bureaucratic system to deal with the disputes of a contentious people. But this pragmatic outcome does not exhaust the possible meanings of his complaint. When he recounts the crisis, we hear the pathos of his repeated *levadi—on my own, alone*—and of his sense of bearing an impossible burden. The imagery of weight-bearing, as of a physical strain, conveys the intimate reality of his experience, as a body responsible for other bodies.

We are reminded of the beginning of the wilderness journey and of his extraordinary metaphor of the pregnant, birthing, and nursing woman: "Was I impregnated with all this people? Did I give birth to them?—that You should tell me, Carry them in your bosom, as a nursing father carries a suckling child . . . ?" (Num. 11:12). Turning to God in bitter complaint, imagining himself as a woman straining under the burdens of her biological role, Moses conveys the experience of the female body given over to the lives of others. He imagines his body changed to accommodate a relationship that is not only unbearable but also unthinkable. He addresses his protest to God, who has imposed this bizarre role upon him: "Why have You done evil to Your servant . . . that You have laid the burden of all this people upon me?" (11:11). Then, God responds by having Moses appoint seventy elders to share the administrative burden.

In his last speeches, however, Moses addresses the people, re-evoking his lonely, visceral resistance to the burden of them. Here, God plays no role: it is Moses who proposes a system whereby "wise, perceptive, and distinguished men" deal with their more immediate issues.

But a different reading of this speech emerges if we imagine Moses as recounting his past complaint with an implicit present demand. What moves him, at this moment, to recall that past moment? How is his present *I* ("I said to you at that time") different from the past *I* ("I can no longer bear you alone! . . . How can I bear unaided the trouble of you . . . ?")

In a poignant Hassidic reading, Mei HaShiloah suggests that Moses is now appealing to his people to acknowledge a past failure. This was a failure in "emotional intelligence." Implicitly, in his past speech, he had wanted them to pray for him that he, and no one but he, should lead them into the Land. At that time, he had realized that God wished to appoint Joshua in his place. Without their prayer—alone, unaided—he would not be able to lead them to their destination. His speech at that time had performed his solitude, his helplessness, and his appeal for their prayers: "I can no longer bear you alone . . ." He had wanted them to respond to his hint—"I need your prayers now!" Moses had wished that the people would want to help him achieve his own desire.

But the people fail to take the hint. They hear only the most obvious meaning of his words, about the bureaucratic burden of his role. They lack *havana*, intuitive understanding.[2] Their obtuseness stains the interaction, and Moses' desire for their desire is left unassuaged. In effect, they confirm his isolation. In this reading, the issue between Moses and the people is his personal desire and disappointment.

Why then does Moses tell the people this story at the beginning of "his own book"? On this reading, overtones of disappointment permeate his story. Perhaps he wants, in this final stage of his interaction with them, to generate in them a sense of how his life is bound up with theirs, in his prayers and in theirs. At that time, he was in their hands; perhaps he in some sense remains in their hands. He intimates his susceptibility to them, to their desires, to their prayers. He is affected by them, in ways that are difficult for them to grasp.

CONFOUNDING VULNERABILITY

What then does he want of them now in this telling? His motive for the narrative is cryptic. The main narrative where this question of motive arises is, of course, his account of God's rejection of his heart's desire: "I beseeched God at that time, saying . . . Let me, I pray, cross over and see the good Land on the other side of the Jordan" (Deut. 3:23–25). He tells the people of his passionate prayer and of God's trenchant repudiation: "Enough! Never speak to Me of this matter again!"

Effectively, God closes his mouth. God had imposed the mission of redemption—of *speaking*—on him in the first place. From the beginning, Moses had replied, "I am not a man of words" (Ex. 4:10). More than that, he had used words graphically to convey his wordlessness: "I am heavy of mouth and heavy of tongue." And, "I am of uncircumcised lips" (6:12, 30).

His subjective sense of intimate weights on mouth, tongue, lips, of burdens, blocks, was countered by God's insistence. But now, it is God who blocks him: no more speaking to Me of this matter!

This is the story that Moses tells his people. Why would he want them to know of his harshest moment of frustration— God's curt dismissal of his words? *"God would not listen to me . . ."* His narrative is the only source of information about this intimate moment. Why does Moses choose to reveal such a painful narrative to his people, as well as to generations of future readers?

In both these narratives, a confounding vulnerability is played out in front of the people. In the last months of his life, Moses expresses himself in a new and personal way to the people whom he has in the past commanded, reproached, exhorted. What is this new timbre of voice, and why does it make itself heard now?

DEAF EARS

We have already noticed (see chapter 2) that the strange image "of uncircumcised lips" describes an *excess*, an "impediment," in the Latin sense of "excess baggage." Something needs to be removed; a foreskin needs to be circumcised. How is this surgery to be achieved? And what motivates him to clear a space for words?

We suggested that Moses is moved by a passion to speak, in the midrashic phrase, *b'shvil yisrael*—for the sake of Israel, and, even more, *on Israel's behalf.* His people have been struck dumb by the traumas of Egypt; they are incapable of testifying for themselves. Primo Levi's dark statement *"We are not the true witnesses"* intimates for us the urgency of Moses' repeated intercessions for his people. The burden of unexpressed national pain, of what kabbalistic sources call *galut ha-dibbur* (the exile of the word), makes him responsible to speak "for Israel," the people's strangled voices shifting the weights in his mouth.

These feats of speech-by-proxy are his spontaneous response to God's angry death sentences against the people. He speaks to God, to good effect, for and on behalf of his people. But God had specifically asked him for a different kind of speech—to act as *His* proxy to Pharaoh and to the people. On this vector, it seems, the impediments that seal his mouth remain largely in place.

Repeatedly, he fails to penetrate Pharaoh's deafness; "Pharaoh would not listen to them" becomes a refrain of the confrontations between them. With these words, plagues and punishments are visited upon the Egyptians, while Pharaoh's heart only hardens with each assault. Moses' words fall on deaf ears till shortly before the end of the story.

As for his people, throughout the journey in the wilderness, he all too often silently enacts his despair in the face of the people's querulousness. He "falls on his face" four times in the book of Numbers. On these occasions, his face in the sand, he dramatically stages what it is to be at a loss for words.

In the narrative of the Spies, for instance, in the crisis of a national death wish, when the people are ready to replace him and return to Egypt (Num. 14:4), Moses and Aaron leave to Caleb and Joshua the task of responding to the rebels (14:5–9). And when Moses does address the people in situations of national crisis, as in the Korach rebellion, he receives no real response. In this context, too, his words fall on deaf ears (16:5–14). Even the sarcastic response of Datan and Aviram highlights the ongoing motif of Moses' sensed ineffectiveness: "Moses was very angry" (16:15) is read by Rashi as "He was very distressed." This is the lifelong distress of one who knows himself unheard by his people.[3]

WORDS, TOUCH, BLOWS

Here, then, is the paradox of Moses' life with words. While his intercessions with God "on behalf of Israel" are eloquent and effective, his interactions with the people are often curt, angry, adversarial. His ease of communication with God throws into high relief the thwarted nature of his exchanges with his people. Only in the human context does he audibly stammer.

But is his speech problem actually a stammer? There seem to be two main theories among the classic commentaries of the Torah text. One is that he complains simply of a lack of eloquence: over his many years of absence in Midian he has lost his mastery of the Egyptian language—he no longer feels equipped to impress Pharaoh with his sophisticated discourse.[4] The other possibility is that he has organic difficulty in pronouncing certain sounds.[5] One indication for this view is God's response to Moses' complaint: "Who gives a man speech? Who makes him dumb . . . ?" (Ex. 4:11).

We notice that the classic commentaries tend to minimize Moses' speech problem, regardless of whether it is organic or cultural: he is simply not as eloquent as he needs to be if he is to act as God's spokesman; he is not good with words. By contrast, the rabbinic literature seems to understand Moses' speech issue as more radical. We have suggested that the early conditions of Moses' life may have created a split in identity and, thus, a confusion of tongues. If we read the text describing Moses' birth and infancy through the prism of midrashic commentary, we come up with a "thicker" version of the origins of his language difficulty—one that supports a psychoanalytic reading.

This story begins with Pharaoh's decree against male Hebrew births. Although the midwives have triumphed in facilitating the birth of baby boys, this only serves to exacerbate the genocidal atmosphere. Now, Pharaoh commands *all* his people to throw *all* male newborns into the river.[6] In this atmosphere, a man from the house of Levi "takes" a daughter of Levi: in the midrashic reading, he *remarries* her, after he has divorced her in despair at the genocidal laws—and all other Israelite couples follow suit, separating and reuniting. His daughter Miriam persuades him to undertake this remarriage by reproaching him for exceeding the rigor of Pharaoh's decree: "Pharaoh decreed only against male infants but your decree prevents any child from being born!"

The baby Moses is born into a world that wants him dead. But his mother "sees that he is good" (beautiful, radiant with transcendent light) and *hides* him for three months. She then takes a basket, seals it, *places* the child in it, and *places* it in the reeds of the river. The princess comes down to the river and *sees* the basket and sends her *amah* to *take* it. What is *amah?* Most obviously, her maidservant. But also, Rashi adds, "her hand— which was miraculously lengthened by many cubits (*amot*), so that she could reach the basket."

It is at this point that we begin to notice the prevalence of hands and handling in this early life story. There is taking and placing and hiding. This child—like all children—is received into a world of waiting hands, all feminine. Helpless, with no control over the conditions of his handling, the infant is touched and held by a world that he did not choose. Before he ever acts, he is acted upon.

Before he even issues his first significant wail, he is *seen*, by his mother and by Pharaoh's daughter, who first sees the basket in the river, then opens it and sees the child who starts wailing. It is the face-to-face impact of the crying child that arouses her compassion, and her recognition of his Hebrew origin. Her seeing, then, extends beyond the immediate scene: it makes connections; it becomes compassionate insight into the fate of Hebrew babies in general.

In addition, the child's wail strikes her as the cry of a much older child—a *na'ar*, a youth. She recognizes a precocious, symbolic power in this infant voice. In midrashic sources, she senses the Israelite tragedy implicit in the scene;[7] or she sees the Shechina, the divine Presence, hovering over the scene.[8] At this point, Moses' sister addresses Pharaoh's daughter and offers to bring her a Hebrew wet nurse. She brings the baby's mother to suckle the baby for Pharaoh's daughter. The relationships are dense with ambiguity: a sister and a daughter and a mother—all unnamed—negotiate in and around their given identities, recognized and unrecognized. Finally, the princess tells Moses' mother to *take* the child away and *nurse* it for her. "And the woman *takes* the child and *nurses* it."

The question of the growth and development of a human being is central to this narrative. In particular, this early life story focuses implicitly on Moses' birth into tactile being. It is only as a result of all this handling, tender, anonymous, and feminine, that he survives and is able to grow.

Twice, we read that Moses "grew": once, when he is weaned and *brought* to Pharaoh's daughter for naming and rearing as her own son; and again, when in the course of time, Moses *emerges* from the palace and *sees* his brothers' suffering.

In fact, his first act in the world is this *va-yeitzei*, this emerging, which opens up new vistas for seeing: he *sees* their suffering, he *sees* the Egyptian beating the Hebrew, he *sees* that there are no witnesses, and he strikes down the Egyptian and buries him in the sand. Eyes and hands now characterize him as a sentient and active being. But this first use of his hand is violent—an oblique act of identification with his brothers. The next day, he again "emerges," this time to *see* two Hebrews fighting and to speak his first words: "Why would you strike your fellow?" (2:13). Already, the enigma of violence among his own people undermines the ethical simplicity of the previous day.

However, the relational matrix in which he has been reared has held its own complexity. He has been moved back and forth between the different touches of his two mothers. His new

Egyptian mother, speculates the Talmud, would first have sought an Egyptian wet nurse for him; but *lo yanak*—he refused to suckle! In a most un-infantlike manner, he turns away from offered breasts. God explains, "How can the mouth that is destined to speak with God suckle impure milk!"⁹ It is only in response to this crisis that Miriam suggests a "wet nurse from among the Hebrews" (2:7).

Withdrawing from the touch of the impure world, Moses manifests susceptibility beyond his years. He is destined for a "mouth-to-mouth" relationship with the divine; even in infancy, he is attuned to that destiny. Moses is already too knowing, already, in a sense, writing his own book.

As we have seen, the Talmud tells another story about the newborn: an angel strikes it on the mouth and makes it forget "the entire Torah" that it knew in the womb.¹⁰ At the same time, remarks Maharal, the angelic touch opens the mouth to language that will reconstruct what has been forgotten. This is what makes the newborn properly human. There is a suggestion here of the rupture, the wound of language: of a loss, a neediness of the body, of its impressionability and its quest for control and connection. Language rushes in to compensate for primal losses. But this critical moment of birth into a complex humanity, suggests Maharal, was never experienced by Moses. His relationship to language—to his mouth—is, in some radical way, different from that of other human beings.

Nevertheless, even as he refuses to suckle, he has already been held in the hands of others. Even as he emerges and acts in the world, forming himself, he has already been formed by others. Before he begins to touch, to strike out at the world, he has been touched.

Moses is affected by the world, even as he affects it. In a climate of violence, of blows and blood, he and Aharon strike the Egyptian river till it bleeds; he brings the plagues, the *makkot* (blows), on the Egyptian people. He strikes the Red Sea and splits it. And, in the end, he strikes the rock at Meriva, thus stalling, as it turns out, a vital process of touching his people to holiness and faith. In God's words, it is "because you have not trusted Me, to sanctify Me before the eyes of the Israelites" (Num. 20:12), that he will not enter the Holy Land. Instead of soft words, he has used angry blows—a failure in touch.

WORDS AS BLUNT WEAPONS

Moses' life with words comes to its crisis when God commands him, "Take the staff, gather the community, you and your brother Aaron, and speak to the rock before their eyes, so that it gives forth its water; and you shall bring forth for them water from the rock and give the community and their cattle to drink" (Num. 20:8). The time is toward the end of the forty-year journey; the people are again bitterly complaining about "no water to drink" (20:5). God's instructions are ambiguous: Moses is to *take the staff*—but to *speak* to the rock. This is different from the previous narrative of water-from-the-rock, thirty-eight years earlier, when he had been told, unequivocally, to *strike* the rock in order to produce water (Ex. 17:6).

The shock effect of the later narrative is delayed to the end. After Moses twice strikes the rock, water issues forth vigorously and the people drink. It is then that God unexpectedly turns to Moses and decrees that he will not enter the Land: "Because you did not trust Me to sanctify Me before the eyes of the Israelites, therefore you shall not bring this community into the land that I have given them" (Num. 20:12).

Astonishingly, God's anger is turned, not against the people for their complaint, but against Moses and Aaron. What is their failure? On the face of it, Moses has succeeded: water has issued from the rock, and the people have quenched their thirst. But God brings a strange viewpoint to the action. This is a failure, He says, in speaking before the *eyes* of the people.

There was a dramatic, *visual* power to be revealed in the act of speaking to the rock; this would have deepened the people's trust in God: "You have failed to *create trust* by sanctifying Me *before their eyes*."

What God wanted of Moses was subtly expressed in His command: not simply that water should issue forth, but that Moses should bring it forth, *elicit* it from the hard rock—*for them*; that, in tenderness and care for his people, he should touch them by touching the rock with his words, rather than by exercising the brutal power of his hand/staff.

In a classic reading, Rashi comments on the story:

> "If you had spoken to the rock and it had produced water, I should have been sanctified before the eyes of the community: they would have said, If this rock, which does not speak or hear, and has no need for sustenance, fulfills God's word, how much more should we!"[11]

The purpose of speaking rather than striking was to elicit from the people a kind of projective identification with the rock. Demonstrating the power of God's word on an insensible rock would have shocked them into a meditation on their own hearts. They would have become aware of the vulnerability of human flesh, as compared to stony rock; to the heart's *impressionability* to the touch of God's word. Before their eyes, a transformation would have taken place—rock to water—which would have engaged with their own fantasies of inner transformation. Eyes and heart are connected: seeing in this way would have evoked a tactile experience of a primal order.

When Moses strikes the rock, the opportunity for a more dynamic image is lost. One midrash puts it in developmental terms:

> When a child is small, his teacher hits him and educates him. But when he grows up, he corrects him with words. So God said to Moses: When this rock was young, you struck it, as it

is said, "And you shall strike the rock . . ." (Ex. 17:6). But now, "You shall speak to the rock"—Recite over it a chapter of Torah and that will produce water from the rock![12]

The people are more mature now; a new generation can be handled in subtler ways. A chapter of Torah will affect them more deeply than the crude impact of a stick. Now, their stony heart is capable of softening into flesh.

Other commentaries take this dichotomy of the word and the blow to a more sensitive place. It is not Moses' use of the staff that is the problem; it is his use of *words*. It is his words of anger to the people: "Listen now, you rebels, shall we produce for you water from this rock?" He is *striking* the people with his words—wielding words as blunt weapons.

This is the reading of Ha'amek Davar. Anger drives Moses off course, as it has before. What was wanted of him was a *soft* use of words. His use of sacred words would have touched and transformed them. Touching them, it would have *taken* them to another place. "All language," writes Emerson, "is vehicular and transitive, and is good, as ferries and horses are, for conveyance, not as farms and houses are, for homestead." Language "can lead me thither where I would be."[13]

The faith or trust (*emuna*) that Moses has sadly failed to elicit from them is an experience of *being drawn* after God, by His word alone. Maharal offers this description of the experience of *emuna:* being drawn by language, one knows joy and freedom. Again, we notice the tactile, kinetic imagery. The human heart is an embodied heart, susceptible to touch and motion.

One has the sense that God is not judging Moses for a one-time failure. His life of leadership has been characterized by a certain "hardness" in his relation to the people. While he passionately advocates *for* them to God, he often speaks *to* them with a kind of repressed anger.

The most dramatic moment in this history is, of course, the moment when Moses smashes the stone tablets "before the eyes of all Israel" (Deut. 34:12). Here, his hand achieves its most powerful act of destruction. This same hand received these tablets from God at the top of the mountain; in the end, this hand will write, or engrave, the second set of tablets, as well as particular segments of the Torah. In writing, his hands will express their power to *subject*—to throw the subject down onto the blank page (or stone block).

These same hands have also been spread in prayer, on a hilltop overlooking the battle with Amalek. Palms open to heaven, he has affected the people's hearts; the gesture of prayer that relinquishes power becomes the essential gesture of the narrative. "And his hands were *emuna*—stable in their prayerful trust."[14] In this position, he grasps at nothing.

But in breaking the Tablets, Moses' underlying anger seems to have its way. Paradoxically, this moment of smashing is implicitly recorded in the last words of the Torah:

> Never again did there arise in Israel a prophet like Moses—whom God knew face to face, for the various signs and portents that God sent him to display in the land of Egypt, against Pharaoh and all his courtiers and his whole country, and for all the great might and awesome power that Moses displayed *before the eyes of all Israel*. (34:10–12)

The Torah summarizes Moses' history of manifest miracles, visible to all. Rashi quotes the Talmud and other sources:

> "*Before the eyes* of all Israel": that he was inspired to smash the Tablets *before their eyes*, as it is said, "And I smashed them *before your eyes*" (9:17). And God assented to Moses' act, as it is said, "[the Tablets] which you smashed" (10:2)—"More power to you that you smashed them!"

Rashi focuses on Moses' hands, which manifest their supreme strength "before the eyes of all Israel," when they smash the stone Tablets they themselves had received from God. Shockingly, God acknowledges Moses' act: "More power to you that you smashed them!"[15] This is the true climax of Moses' prodigious life, validated and blessed by God. He is inspired (lit., his heart lifted him up) to this spontaneous and violent gesture. Where is the blessing in such a destructive moment?

Stone Tablets inscribed by the finger of God are a magnificent image for permanence. To smash these tablets is evidently to destroy the assurance of permanence. The Talmud expresses the idea: "If the Tablets had not been smashed, the Torah would never have been forgotten by Israel."[16] The stony object with its engraved letters represents the Written Torah—forever preserved, subjected. As an image for the unforgettable, the Tablets must give way to the life of human beings, who "learn and forget."[17]

After they are smashed, the life of the Oral Torah begins. As Moses constantly warns the people, to forget the Torah is, on the one hand, the worst risk of their future history. On the other hand, unmaking what has been made may release the object to translation, to unconscious transformations, elaborating it in a world of diffuse impressions. In a word, forgetting generates interpretation. Smashing the stony writing restores it to its elements, to its godly, human potential. Unmaking things gives value to our making. Ultimately, unmaking, forgetting clears space for human creativity.

Moses' strange masterpiece, then, is an act of sublimating his anger in order to make room for his people's future life with God's words. Before their eyes, he *lets fly:* he lets the letters fly off the stone. The last words of the Torah—"before the eyes of all Israel" (*l'einei kol yisrael*)—as read in the oral traditions of interpretation, refer to this moment and imply God's blessing of the act: "More power to you that you smashed them!" Moses'

last written words implicitly celebrate the dissolution of written words: they are an apotheosis in which his anger is turned
in a movement of release.

The significance of the Meriva story can be appreciated
only in the context of Moses' life with his people. At Meriva,
he failed to find the blessing in the touch of words. He was to
have elicited from his people their visionary capacity, their susceptibility to impressions remaining after the visible has disappeared. Impressionism, we remember, was the name given to a
group of painters who tried to represent what is "left behind"
when the scene has vanished. The Impressionist painting "is
painted in such a way that *you are compelled to recognize that it
is no longer there.*"[18]

The scene by the rock was to have been something of an
"Impressionist" moment. The rock will disappear, like the stone
Tablets, but those who witness divine words drawing forth
water may retain impressions, traces infused with other traces.
So trust may spring from deep within.

This is the power of the metaphor of water emerging from
rock. As distinct from other possible metaphors—heavy rains
falling from leaden skies or rising from deep underground
springs—this image yields an *internal* sense of the stony heart
evolving into impressionable flesh. What emerges is *emergence*
itself—gentle, organic revelation—under the impact of words.
This reverie evokes the possibility of a new, more responsive
nature opening in the heart.

WHO AM I?

Through what Moses fails to do we understand something
of what was possible. In the space between Moses and Israel, a
potentiality remains to be tapped. We also intuit something of

the deep anger that sometimes hardens Moses' heart in his relation to his people. Impacted within that anger is the life of a man
who was born into a world that wanted him dead; to a mother
whose hands held him sporadically and in tension with the claim
of another mother; and to a people with whom he is ill at ease.

At the Burning Bush, this man Moses is sought by God.
He responds with a full *Hineni—Here I am!* Even before the
Burning Bush—from the beginning, when he kills the Egyptian taskmaster, or when he drives away the harassing Midianite shepherds (Ex. 2:17)—he has responded to ethical demands
as though they were unavoidable.

At the same time, in the next breath, he answers God's call
with a question about the *I*—"Moses! Moses!"—who is being
called: "Who am I?" (*Mi anochi* [3:11]). He pleads inadequacy to
the role of redeemer, of God's spokesman to Pharaoh and to his
newfound brothers. "Who am I that I should go to Pharaoh
and free (*otzi*) the Israelites from Egypt?" How does one per-
suade a slave people to *emerge* from slavery? How does one
emerge from one's own complexity and act in the world? How
does one draw water from a rock?[19]

At this stage, Moses cannot envisage his own role in the
world. So God answers him: "I will be with you" (3:12). We notice that God singles out Moses' *anochi*, his *I* ("Who am I?") to
trigger His own *Anochi*—"*I* will be with you." It is not Moses'
social discomfort or inadequacy alone that God addresses, but
a more vulnerable inwardness that connects his *anochi* with
deep sources of being. "*I* will be with you": being with God
means being animated by the divine force of an *I* that is and is
not one's own selfhood.

BEYOND WORDS AND FACES

What we witness after this moment at the Burning Bush
is the singular intimacy of Moses' relation with God, as well as

the more troubled narrative of his relation with the people. At the heart of his relation with God is a dynamic in which the anger of his life finds intimate expression. This appears most clearly in midrashic accounts of his interactions with God, *for the sake of Israel.* Here is a dramatic example of this genre of intervention narrative:

> "And Moses entreated before the Lord his God" (32:11). R. Tanchuma b. Abba began thus: "Therefore He spoke of destroying them, if Moses His chosen one had not stood in the breach before Him, to avert His anger" (Ps. 106:23). R. Hama b. Hanina said: The good advocate knows how to present his case clearly before the tribunal. Moses was one of two advocates that arose to defend Israel and set themselves, as it were, against God. These were Moses and Daniel. That Moses was one we deduce from: "if Moses His chosen had not stood in the breach." . . . These were the two men who set their face against the attribute of strict justice in order to plead for mercy on Israel's behalf.
>
> R. Berachya said two things, one in the name of Rabbenu and the other in the name of R. Samuel b. Nahman. Rabbenu said: It can be compared to a king who was sitting in judgment on his son, while the prosecutor was indicting him. When the prince's tutor saw that his pupil was being condemned, he pushed the prosecutor outside the court and put himself in his place in order to plead on the prince's behalf. Similarly, when Israel made the Golden Calf, Satan stood within (before God) accusing them, while Moses was outside. What did Moses do? He arose and pushed Satan out and put himself in his place, as it says, "If His chosen one had not stood in the breach before Him"—that is, he put himself in place of him who was causing the breach.
>
> R. Samuel b. Nahman said: It is difficult to say that he "stood in the breach before Him." It can be explained by the case of a king who was angry with his son and took his place on the tribunal and tried him and pronounced him guilty. As

he was about to take up the pen to sign the verdict, his associate snatched the pen from his hand in order to appease his
anger. Similarly, when Israel committed that act, God sat in
judgment upon them to condemn them, for it says, "Let Me
alone, that I may destroy them" (Deut. 9:14). But He had not
yet done so, but was about to seal their decree, as it says, "He
that sacrifices to the gods, except to God alone, shall be utterly destroyed" (Ex. 22:19). So what did Moses do? He took
the Tablets from God's hands in order to avert His anger.

This can be compared to a king who sent a marriage
broker to betroth a wife to him, but while the broker was on
his way, the woman offended with another man. What did
the broker, who was entirely innocent, do? He took the marriage document that the king had given him to betroth her
with and tore it up, saying: "It is better that she be judged as
an unmarried woman rather than as a married woman." This
is what Moses did; when Israel committed that act, he took
the Tables and shattered them, as if to imply that had Israel
foreseen the punishment awaiting them, they would not have
sinned. Moreover, Moses said: "Better that they be judged as
unintentional sinners than as willful sinners"—because in
the Decalogue it says, "I am the Lord your God," and the
punishment for breaking this commandment is: "He that
sacrifices to the gods, except to God alone, shall be utterly
destroyed." Therefore he broke the Tablets.

"And He spoke of destroying them": Immediately,
Moses girded his loins for prayer. That is the meaning of
"And Moses entreated [*Va-yichal*] before the Lord his God."
He placed himself in God's presence with scant respect [a
wordplay on *Va-yichal* and *chulin*] in order to request Israel's
needs. Hence, "And Moses entreated before the Lord his
God."[20]

Moses acts as a good "defense counsel" for Israel, when
God is about to destroy them after the sin of the Golden Calf.
But the passage begins with a series of wordplays on "face,"

panim. The proof-text, we notice, is "And Moses entreated before the *face* of God" (32:11). R. Tanchuma cites another proof-text: "He spoke of destroying them, if Moses His chosen one had not stood in the breach before Him (before His *face*)" (Ps. 106:23). R. Chuna defines the good advocate as one who explains, clarifies the *face* (*masbir panim*) of his case before the tribunal. Moses' advocacy consists of "setting his *face*" (*ma'amid panim*),[21] as it were, against God. He sets his *face* (*natan panav*) against the divine attribute of strict justice.

It seems that advocacy involves putting the best possible face, the most plausible construction, on the case, resisting the inexorable claim of strict justice. *Panim* literally means "faces, facets," in the plural. A face, in Hebrew, has plural implications, a shifting mosaic of facets—"to prepare a face to meet the faces that you meet."[22]

Three parables follow. In the first, the prince's tutor intervenes when the prosecuting counsel seems to be prevailing: he rudely pushes the prosecuting counsel off his dais in court and stands in his place in order to defend the prince. So, R. Berachya says, Moses pushes Satan, who is effectively attacking the Israelites, out of his place *inside* (*b'fnim*) the court. He then stands in Satan's place.

The second rabbinic parable tells of an angry king who is just about to sign the verdict condemning his son, when his "associate" (*sunkatedro*) snatches the pen out of his hand *to avert his anger.* So God is about to sign the death warrant against Israel when Moses seizes the stone tablets (the text that proscribes the sin of idolatry) in order *to avert His anger.*

A third parable involves a wife instead of a son. The lady offends her husband-to-be just when the marriage broker is on his way to betroth her to the king. The broker saves the situation by tearing up the marriage document, destroying the text that would have condemned her. In this way, she can claim ignorance of the requirements of marriage. So Moses shatters the Tablets, thus giving Israel the pretext of ignorance.

In the last section, the expression *Va-yichal* ("Moses entreated God") is read: he acted unceremoniously, with scant respect (*chol* meaning profanely, brazenly) for God: "He stood in (lit.) *light-headedness* before the face of God to ask for the needs of Israel." Here again, it is the face with which Moses faces God that lends a dramatic, even a theatrical aspect to the encounter.

In this arresting midrash, the rabbis are, in effect, interpreting the nature of Moses' face-to-face relation with God. "And God would speak face-to-face to Moses, as a man speaks to his friend" (Ex. 33:11). To speak face-to-face is clearly different from *seeing God's face*, which, as we discover a few verses later, is the further intimacy that Moses requests and is denied (33:20). To speak face-to-face is to adopt a face, one of many possible facets of a relationship. In order to advocate for Israel, Moses unceremoniously puts on a hostile face, in order to stand *against* God's face of strict justice.

As the parables proceed, Moses' role-playing becomes more violent. At first, he opposes God, "as it were." Then, without apology, he opposes God's justice. Then, he pushes the prosecution counsel out of court and takes his place. Then, he seizes the pen from the king's hand. Finally, he tears up the betrothal document.

What gives Moses license to behave in such a vigilante manner? Particularly surprising is the dramatic detail of replacing the prosecutor inside the court: in effect, Moses is changing places with Satan, from an external to an intimate position (before the king's face). By a kind of sleight of hand, he substitutes himself for Satan and defends the people from a "satanic" (aggressive, oppositional) place.

Strikingly, the midrash calls Moses "the king's *associate*."

Moses knows that he has an ally in God. Beneath the judicial formalities, there is an affinity that connects God and Moses. Both are interested in the vindication and survival of Israel (the king's son). Moses knows, even as he puts his most aggressive face forward, that he is serving the divine desire in defending Israel. This collusiveness with God allows Moses to play roles, as in a human encounter, where one reads the ambivalence of the other, intuitively eliciting his most loving self. The dynamics of an intimate relationship are called into play.

This audacious dynamic lies at the heart of many rabbinic interpretations of the biblical text. Moses acts as His Majesty's Loyal Opposition, as Yochanan Muffs aptly terms it.[23] He has, in a sense, internalized the function of prosecutor, the angry, antagonistic role; he uses his anger in order to "avert God's anger."

His lifelong anger, in this case, finds a way of acting in the interest of compassion. In another striking Talmudic passage, Moses ascends to the higher worlds, only to have God reprimand him: "Moses, don't they say Shalom [Good morning!] where you come from?" Moses answers, "Master of the Universe, does a servant say Shalom to his master?" God then says, "You should have helped Me!" (Rashi comments: "You should have said, May You succeed in Your work!") Immediately, Moses responds, "Now, may the divine power grow greater!"[24]

Moses' intimacy with God transforms his modesty into an enactment of his power to "help" God. He is God's servant, but, like one who speaks with his friend, he intuits what kind of conversation God desires. He mobilizes his deepest resources, sometimes of anger, against the divine forces of destruction.

Divine anger plays a large role in the biblical imagination. What can a human being do in the face of this anger, if not use his own knowledge of anger to move God from one place to another? The image of the father's anger with his son is a midrashic commonplace; fathers notoriously tend to become enraged. What is needed is an intercessor, who cares for both father and son, who will know how to soothe the paternal fury.

Moses knows about anger; it is not hard for him to enter into the role of Satan, the Accuser. In this role, he becomes aggressively masculine: pushing, snatching, tearing, girding his loins. Here, it seems, is "Moses, the man" in full force, taking charge of the relationship. And yet this masculine persona is only one aspect of the situation. It is equally true that his role is played in order to "ask for the needs of Israel," as the midrash points out. Moses, however assertive, is nevertheless in the position that is attributed to the *wife* who asks/demands the household expenses from her husband. In pleading for the existential needs of his people, Moses is playing a distinctly feminine role.

In other words, his relation with God embraces both the power and the powerlessness of his intimacy with the divine. In transcending the formal postures of "feminine" behavior, he plays roles that are expressive of the full range of a relationship face-to-face with God. He is, in fact, playing out the implications of his own question, "Who am I?" In context, the question has a limited reference: "Who am I that I should go to Pharaoh and bring the Israelites out of Egypt?" But, in addition to this obvious self-deprecating meaning, "Who am I?" stands alone as a starkly existential question. This is, for Moses, *the* question: "Who is the *I* who is being called?"

"MOST BEAUTIFUL OF WOMEN"

Face-to-face with God, Moses is both masculine and feminine. In rabbinic parable, his assertiveness, his unceremonious behavior, his girding his loins in prayer—these constitute precisely the persona of the wife making demands of her husband, for and on behalf of her household. In the midrashic imagination, Moses becomes "most beautiful among women" (Song of Songs 1:8):

Most beautiful of prophets, most excellent of prophets! [I.e., Moses] Why are the prophets compared to women? Just as a woman is not shy to demand of her husband the needs of her household, so the prophets are not shy to demand the needs of Israel of their Father in heaven.[25]

The "feminine" character of prophets is expressed by their bold demands of God who, like the man of the house, is personally implicated in the welfare of his family. Moses' "wifely" understanding of God's intimate concern for his people allows him a bold range of behaviors. In the end, the differences between typically masculine and feminine, aggressive and submissive behaviors blur in the light of a larger vision: these are, after all, roles played in the interest of a common passion.

So Moses stages his anger in order to avert God's anger. His concern for Israel is ultimately at one with his connection with God. Most excellent of prophets, Moses becomes in the rabbinic imagination the paradigm of the human being who is emboldened in his very humanity. The feminine figure of Ruth—the solitary stranger who makes her demands of the rich landowner—comes to mind. At the end of the night on the granary floor, she "girds her loins like a male,"[26] with six ears of corn in her kerchief, and returns to Naomi (Ruth 3:15). In calling her a "woman of valor" (3:11), Boaz recognizes her as transcending the stereotypes of male and female, like the "woman of valor" in Proverbs 31:17: "She girds her loins in strength."

Simple gender distinctions are blurred in Moses' self-presentation. Many rabbinic narratives play out the implications of his "wife-prophet" identity. But we remember the question that Moses asked at the Burning Bush: "Who am I?" immediately following on "Here I am!" In Moses' speculations about his relation to the people, the question persists. His body becomes the subject of outrageous fantasies: pregnant, birthing, suckling and bearing his people, a feminine persona emerges from the shadows, appalling and yet strangely necessary to imagining an unimaginable role. A new *I* is in the process of being born; and as in all births, the nascent self encounters resistance.

FEMINIZATIONS

Only in his interventions with God in defense of the people does Moses enact his role with unabashed force. In his connection with God, he knows that this masculine/feminine persona is the effect of his total concern for the *bayit*—the household of Israel—which is, ultimately, both his and God's. Face to face with God, he is free to express an adversary loyalty to God's true desire.

For it is a *bayit* that, ultimately, God and Moses are building. In midrashic narratives, God's desire is to live among these Israelites, in their midst, within them.[27] This interiority is to be characterized, writes Emanuel Levinas, by a welcoming of the face of the Other, who reveals himself "not in a shock negating the I, but as the primordial phenomenon of gentleness."[28] This gentleness, this peaceable welcome is found "in the gentleness of the feminine face."

Gentleness ("douceur") as the primordial ground of meeting with the Other is implicit in the "feminine" face of the prophets, and especially of Moses. His intimacy with God can only be represented by the intimacy of marriage, or of two friends who speak to one another. These intimacies contain an infinity and invoke a radiant separateness.

It is, therefore, largely in his encounters with the Other who is God that Moses comes to know and feel his own humanity. The concern of these encounters is, most potently, the people who are the "household" of mutual concern. However, when Moses encounters the people themselves, the story becomes much more complicated. Here, the Rabbis intuit that he sometimes feels "as weak as a female."[29] Here, he struggles with a "feminization" of his being that is experienced as a helplessness: the people are doomed beyond any possibility of salvation. At such moments, he is thrown back to an infant dependency on the touch of others. How can he be the powerful mother if his primal being is that of the infant, speechless and susceptible? "Weak as a woman" is indeed the weakest and least imaginative of the associations of femininity. The female shares with the infant a moment where agency totally fails.

HIS OWN BOOK

It is against this background that Moses' final speeches in Deuteronomy stand out in high relief. In these autobiographical speeches, a complex *I* for the first time appears in the biblical text. As he recounts the events of the last forty years, he constructs, from his present perspective, the narratives of the past. *Shema yisrael,* "Hear o Israel," he says, in his own voice, exhorting the people *now* and *here* to internalize and teach others what was undergone many years ago: laws were given and dramas played out *in those days* and *in that time,* in which *I* played a key role.[30] In saying *I,* over and over, Moses gives an account of himself that effectively creates his past self. As a feeling, knowing person, he is giving birth to himself in this new *I;* he is answering his own original question, "Who am I?"

When the Talmud declares that Moses "wrote his own book," therefore, it suggests that he wrote this book of Deuteronomy with a singularly intimate intent. It is "his own book" because in it his *I* is animated to feel and know as never before. In this, as in so much else, he plays out the implicit tensions of his people's narrative. For the first time, he cites himself with a sense of his implication in their dilemmas.

AMAZING INSENTIENCE

One particularly poignant moment of this kind comes toward the end when he reproaches the people, "God has not given you a heart to know, or eyes to see, or ears to hear, until this day" (Deut. 29:3).

For forty years, he has led the people through the wilderness. But it is only now that he can articulate their tragic flaw: their lack of *sentience*. Only now, retrospectively, can Moses speak, not only of obedience and disobedience, faith and skepticism, but also of the heart, the eyes, and the ears that are unaccountably absent from their body experience. Their senses, their ability to be affected by the world, are somehow deficient.

This is his last speech before they enter the Covenant, which ends the Torah narrative. He has just spoken of all the great signs and wonders that their eyes have seen, even repeating the expression, "that your eyes have seen" (29:2). Why, then, does he add this personal, scathing coda about their amazing insentience over the forty years of his leadership? Perhaps, suggests the Talmud, he is referring to a developmental capacity—for gratitude—that only "this day" has finally evolved: "From here we learn," says Rava, "that one does not fully understand one's teacher until forty years have passed."[31]

Rava reads hopefully, against the grain of the text. It is the emotional and moral resonances of one's teacher's Torah that may take forty years to realize. Rashi adds: "Till this very day" suggests that "this day you have become a people!" (29:6). Now, they are responsible for their own moral being.[32] Moses has granted the people forty years of latitude; now begins their time of full moral responsibility. Their past deficits are part of their process of maturation.

However, in another comment, Rashi goes further: "*God has not given you a heart to know:* to recognize God's loving acts and to cling to Him. *Till this very day:* this day I understand that you do cling to God and desire Him!" Here, the subject is not so much the people's moral development as their passionate vision of God's love and their emotional capacity to love Him in return. Moses criticizes the people for their insentience, and, implicitly, celebrates the radical turn in their relation to God, "this very day."[33] Gratitude and love are now within their range of religious experience.

If the people have indeed changed, then the change can be put down to the fact that this is, in fact, a new generation. When Moses speaks of their past, then, he is often referring to the experience of their parents' generation. *You* is a more slippery reference than it seems. But so, it turns out, is *I*.

"Now, I understand that you do desire God!" Perhaps this new generation is only beginning to desire; perhaps those who cannot see and hear and feel have never been rightly touched. The experience of *tactility* is the ground on which the *I* begins to see, hear, and feel—and to become utterable. Their life as a full *I* begins only at the end of the forty-year wilderness time. Something finally touches them into being, capable ultimately of *knowing from the heart*.

But if there is a deficit in the people's nurturing, Moses is implicated in this failure. He was to have been the nurturing mother who bore them in his bosom (Num. 11:12); that primary *holding* relation of mother and infant never quite happened. Moses' personal history not only affects his relation with his people but also dramatically plays out the implicit tensions of their national history.

Handed back and forth between two mothers, drawn out of the deathly river to become a son to the Egyptian princess, while his true mother is forced to abandon him, Moses in his infancy is held in close focus. This is the ground of his life: fraught with loss, formed by the will of the powerful and the helplessness of the weak, held and relinquished and held and relinquished, until he *emerges* to find his brothers in their humiliation.

If he finds it inconceivable to *hold* this people in the way that he imagines God wants him to do, that is a direct effect of his own earliest history. "Who am I?" becomes a burning question. And when at the end of his life he recognizes a radical deficit in his people, perhaps at the same time he recognizes the ways in which he has not fully held them (*"This day I understand* that you passionately desire God!"*). If they have not developed a certain emotional *knowing,* perhaps this is both a reflection of his own history and a partial effect of it?

But when Moses last addresses the people before the Covenant, he seems to imply that now, "on this day," they have finally developed a knowing heart, seeing eyes, and hearing ears—and that he has developed a new understanding of them. Perhaps this moment also marks a development in himself as leader and nurturer?

How has this development taken place? Why is it that Moses' language in Deuteronomy is now full of references to *love* between the people and God: expressions like *chashak, chafatz, ahav*—desire, wish, love—appear in these last speeches as never before. A new note enters Moses' language. His retellings of their history are animated by a new use of the autobiographic *I.*

INTIMATE NARRATIVES

We can now return to the scene in which Moses tells the people of his frustrated prayer: "Please let me cross over . . ." (Deut. 3:25). We asked why Moses chooses to convey this scene to the people. This painful interchange—"Enough! Never speak to Me of this matter again!"—is never narrated in any other way. What would have been lost if Moses (or the narrator) had quietly suppressed the story? What is gained by communicating this private moment of humiliation?

He not only tells it to the people but then also writes it, at

God's behest, into "his own book." We, generations of readers, know not only what happened between Moses and God but also that Moses chose to communicate this to his listeners and readers, for all time. The final choice is, of course, the narrator's decision to narrate this intimate episode in this way.

Moses' narrative is, I suggest, also a narrative of Moses' initiation into a newly evocative confrontation with his people. Between the lines, he tells another story in which both he and they are implicated in complex and intimate ways. If God told him so curtly, "Never speak to Me of this matter again!" implicitly He was also saying, "Never speak *to Me* . . ."—redirecting Moses' words away from God and toward the people.

We have seen how often Moses has been eloquent and effective in his interventions with God. Now—because the issue concerns his personal desire—God blocks his access to the divine and reframes the situation as a human one. The main issue is not God's decree but the fraught relations between Moses and his people.

In dramatic reconstructions of Moses' speeches, midrashic sources attend to this counternarrative. In these texts, Moses narrates his disappointment, not only with God's response, but also with the people's apathy. The focus of these speeches is personal: Moses strikes an unprecedented note of candor when he reproaches his people for abandoning him in his hour of need.

It is this emotional timbre that animates his many references, for instance, to the theme of "You are crossing over; I am not crossing over": "You shall not cross over; Joshua will cross over" (Deut. 3:27–28); or, "I die in this land, I am not crossing over the Jordan, but you are crossing over" (4:22). What sounds out of these many juxtapositions of his fate and theirs is, according to one midrashic tradition, disappointment, reproach, sadness, anger. Similarly, the final reproach that we have just discussed—"God has not given you a heart to know, eyes to see, ears to hear, till this day . . ."—is read as overwhelmingly *personal.*

Here is one such midrash:

> Therefore, when they came to cross over the Jordan, Moses reminded them of every plea that he had made on their behalf, because he thought that they would pray on his behalf that he should enter the Land with them. What is the force of "You will pass over"? R. Tanchuma said: Moses prostrated himself before Israel and said to them: "You are to pass over, but not I," and he gave them the opportunity [opened an opening for them] to pray for him, but they did not understand him.
>
> This can be compared to a king who had many children by a noble lady. The lady offended him and he resolved to divorce her. He said to her: "Know that I am going to marry another wife." She replied: "Yes, but won't you tell me whom it is you intend to marry?" He replied: "So-and-so." What did the noble lady do? She summoned her children and said to them: "Know that your father intends to divorce me and to marry So-and-so; could you bear being subjected to her?" They replied: "Yes!" She then said: "Know what she will do to you." She thought that perhaps they would understand what she meant and would intercede with their father on her behalf, but they did not understand. As they did not understand, she said: "I will command you only for your own sake—Be mindful of your father's honor!"
>
> So it was with Moses. When God said to him: "Take Joshua the son of Nun . . ." (Num. 27:18); "For you shall not pass over this Jordan" (Deut. 3:27), Moses said to Israel, "And it shall come to pass, when the Lord your God shall bring you into the Land where you are going to possess it" (Deut. 11:29); when he stressed the words, "*You* are to pass over this day [not I]," he thought that perhaps Israel would understand. As they did not understand, he said: "I will command you only for your own sakes; be mindful of the

honor of your Father in heaven." How do we know this?
For it is said, "That you may fear the Lord your God . . ."
(Deut. 6:2).[34]

Here, Moses solicits his people, hinting to them that they
might plead for God's mercy on him. He cannot directly ask
for their prayers that he be allowed to lead them into the Land;
all he can do is "open an opening" for their own spontaneous
understanding. He prostrates himself before them, acting out
his need for their intercession, reminding them of his history
of intercession in their hour of need. But they do not "understand"—*lo hayu mevinim:* intuition is sorely lacking at this point.
Here we have the midrashic background for the Hassidic commentary of Mei HaShiloach that we discussed earlier in this
chapter.

In the rather sardonic parable of the noble lady who pleads
with her children to intervene with their father, the mother
asks leading questions to sensitize them to her danger. But with
amazing obtuseness, they "do not understand"; they fail to "get
it." In the end, she warns them that life with their father and
without her interventions will be difficult for them too. But
they still fail to take the hint.

Why can the noble lady not ask her children directly to intercede with their father for her? Why can Moses not appeal
explicitly for his people's help? This is the delicate nature of the
relationship of the leader with his people: the question of love
and desire, as in the mother/child relation, hangs between them.
"Do you really want me? If you do, you will press my case; you
will help me cross over the Jordan." A fraught relation like that
of Moses and the Israelites is being tested; the people are in-
sensitive to Moses' desire for their desire; they manifest an
emotional immaturity that can only pain Moses.

The fact that the midrash puts him into the specific situation
of a *mother* who is subject to the desires of both her husband

and her children serves, yet again, to play out the "feminine" voice of Moses' identity. Moses' helpless condition—"weak as a woman"—emerges in words of satirical power. This paradox, of constitutive helplessness and literary power, gives bitter personal meaning, as we have suggested, to his final criticism of the people: "God has not given you a heart to know . . .":

Another explanation: "*God has not given you a heart to know*": R. Samuel b. Nahmani said: Moses said this with reference to his own situation. How so? God made two decrees, one affecting Israel, and one affecting Moses. The first was when they committed the unmentionable sin [the Golden Calf]. For it is said, "Let Me alone, that I may destroy them" (Deut. 9:14). The other decree was when Moses sought to enter the Land of Israel and God said to him, "You shall not pass over this Jordan" (Deut. 3:27). Moses therefore entreated God to annul both decrees. He said: "Master of the Universe, Pardon, I pray you, the iniquity of this people according to the greatness of Your lovingkindness" (Num. 14:19) and God's decree was annulled, while Moses' prayer was fulfilled. How do we know this? For it is said, "I have pardoned according to your word" (14:20).

When he was about to enter the Land, Moses entreated: "Let me cross over, I pray You, and see the good Land" (Deut. 3:25). God replied: "Moses, on a former occasion, you annulled My decree and I granted your prayer; I said: 'Let Me destroy them,' and you prayed, 'Pardon, I pray You,' and your prayer was fulfilled. On this occasion, I desire to carry out My decree and to refuse your prayer." God added: "Moses, you do not know how to behave! You wish to hold the rope by both ends! If you insist on My granting 'Let me cross over, I pray You,' then you must withdraw the prayer, 'Pardon, I pray You'; and if you insist on 'Pardon, I pray You,' then you must withdraw, 'Let me pass over, I pray You.'"

R. Joshua b. Levi said: When Moses our teacher heard this, he exclaimed before God: "Master of the Universe, let

Moses and a hundred like perish rather than that the fingernail of even one of them be injured!" R. Samuel b. Isaac said:
When Moses was nearing his end and Israel did not pray for
him that he should enter the Land, he assembled them and
began rebuking them with the words: One man saved sixty
myriads at the time of the Golden Calf, and yet sixty myriads
cannot save one man! This is the force of, "*God has not given
you a heart to know.*"[35]

The people's insentience begins and ends the passage. This
is the proof-text for the theme of Moses' reproach, here called
a *tochacha*, a rebuke. But in this rebuke, Moses is personally
implicated. He speaks not for general principles of proper behavior but out of his own intimate narrative of betrayal by his
people.

He tells a story of his own surrender of his dearest desire in
favor of the people's need. Of his two prayers—"Please forgive
Your people's sin" and "Please let me cross over . . ."—Moses
must choose only one. Unhesitatingly, he chooses to annul the
divine decree against his people, relinquishing his own desire.

His choice is, in a sense, a foregone conclusion. When God
tells him that he cannot overrule the divine decree on both issues, his response is hyperbolic: "Let Moses and a hundred like
him die, rather than one fingernail of even one of them be injured!" A fingernail against a hundred Moseses! This is the narrative he presents to the people, to express his disappointment
at their insensitivity: "God did not give you a heart to know
. . ." The biblical words become vehicles for a painful and personal reproach; they carry a story of sacrificial love to which
the people have failed to respond.

But this story, which brings to light Moses' present understanding of himself—"Who am I?"—is composed in the moment of "rebuke." The rebuke reveals more than perhaps he
knows—not only a critique of the people, but a wounded sense
of himself. Before Moses voices the critique—in this midrashic

version—it is only implicit within the words of the Torah. Now, Moses' speeches reveal, from between the lines of the Torah, a history of unrequited love and grievance. The people have been heartless, blind, and deaf to the implicit meanings of the story. If they had had a heart to know, they might have put this story together for themselves; they might have understood the ethical demand it made on them to pray for Moses.

This kind of address, as "rebuke," involves the speaker in bringing his own life into full, vulnerable presence. *Tochacha* (rebuke) is related to *nocheach*—being present. In the first person, Moses is present before the people: surrendering his own interests for theirs, ironically comparing the ratios of 1 for 600,000 and 600,000 for 1. If he is to reach them in the singular mode of *tochacha*, he must bring the concentrated force of his own history, of his emotional presence, to bear on them.

FOR THE SAKE OF ISRAEL

At this late turning point, Moses, who has always complained to God about the people's deafness—"They will not believe me, nor will they listen to my voice!" (Ex. 4:1)—now complains to the people about God's refusal to listen to him. In the arena where language had failed him—in his connection with his people—he now allows himself to speak with irresistible eloquence and emotional candor.

A passage in Midrash Tanchuma remarks dryly: "Just yesterday, you said, I am not a man of words—and now you have so much to say!"[36] Like springs in the desert, language gushes forth—"These are the words that Moses spoke"—in this last book of the Torah, which is "his own book." But it is not only a matter of the *many* words of these last speeches but of the intimacy and vulnerability of his voice as he tells these stories. In the aftermath of a kind of rupture with God—who, for the first time, refuses to listen to him—Moses turns toward a new conversation with his people. Now, he must use his own imagination, his "understanding," to hear what is not explicitly said. God has closed one door and, implicitly, provokes him to open another door.

This is not, in fact, the first time that God has cut off the conversation between Himself and Moses. According to a midrashic tradition, the thirty-eight years during which the entire generation dies in the wilderness are years in which God does not speak to Moses. In Rashi's words:

> "And God spoke to me" (Deut. 2:17): But from the time of the Spies till now, there is no mention of God's speaking (*va-yidaber*), only of saying (*va-yomer*). This teaches that all 38 years when the people were in disfavor, God did not *speak*— affectionately, face to face, and deliberately—with Moses. This teaches that the divine Presence does not come to rest on the prophet except *for the sake of Israel.*

God's relationship with Moses, unique and intimate as it may be, is only "for the sake of Israel." When the people live in the shadow of death, Moses has no access to the divine. Only after the dying is over (2:16), does God, in the full sense, again *speak* to Moses.

This, too, is part of the message that Moses communicates to the people in his last speeches. God's loving communion is calibrated according to the rhythms of the people's life and death. When God explicitly stops Moses in mid-sentence, it is as though He were redirecting him to another horizon of desire.

SUBLIMATED DESIRE

Strangely, it is precisely after God has finally dashed his hopes of "crossing over" that Moses achieves a new force of language. Rashi situates his aborted prayer at the juncture, in Numbers 27:12, where God, rather mysteriously, commands

Moses to "ascend the Mount of Transitions and look at the land." No prayer is mentioned here, but Rashi senses that God's command is, in fact, His response to Moses' prayer. This definitive command, "Look at it [the Land] and be gathered in to your people . . ." (27:13), is, in effect, a sentence of death.

But immediately following on this, we read, "Moses *spoke* (*va-yidaber*) to God" (27:15). The force and intimacy of *va-yidaber* is nowhere else used in Moses' addresses to God; the invariable form is *va-yomer*, a softer, more modest expression. Why does God's rejection of his prayer release in him such unprecedented verbal energy? Rashi comments: "To teach the praise of the righteous, who when they depart from this world, relinquish their own needs and involve themselves in the needs of the community." The midrash puts it succinctly: "Anyone who speaks for the community, it is as though he comes with force [lit., with the power of his arm]."[37]

At this point, Moses speaks forcefully to God about the appointment of a successor. Silenced on one subject, he speaks aggressively on another. The vector of his desire has shifted. He speaks now to the people and on their behalf with a passion into which his own desire has metaphorically "crossed over."

This too is part of the story that he tells the people. There was, he says, a prayer for himself, which God cut short and he relinquished. That prayer might never have been known, if he had not told his people—who are now the object of his desire—of its thwarting. Where, he implicitly asks, were your prayers for me, or your desire for me, when my prayers were failing?

Instead of a passion to cross over the Jordan, Moses is now possessed by a new passion—to reach across to his people, before he dies. He lays his intimate narrative at their door. What is it precisely that he wants of them?

Where previously he had addressed them in God's name, conveying His messages and commandments, he now addresses them *b'shvil yisrael*, for the sake of Israel, *on behalf* of Israel. His role as God's spokesman shifts to a new register. Now, he speaks without divine authority, in order to bring something new into being. Before, he had said *I* in God's voice, reporting God's will and intention.[38] Now, he utters the *anochi*, the *I*, in order to bring to life another self, intersubjective, not fully known.

UNDERSTANDING IN CHORDS

The "living sounds of speech" are the utterances of poets and storytellers. As Moses recounts the story of his prayer and its thwarting, an *I* is generated in the act of speaking. Something new transpires between Moses and his people. Without preconceiving his meaning, he makes present the unspoken and the unspeakable. What he wants of them, before he dies, is that they experience what it is to understand in chords, to understand simultaneously meanings from a plurality of worlds. That they begin to hear and see with a difference.

For Moses, becoming *Moshe rabbenu* (Moses our teacher, our master) involves a new project of publicly subjecting himself to a learning process, in which the teacher, like the patient in psychoanalysis, testifies to experiences that he does not fully master.[39] This is a literary kind of learning, which can be read, or heard, in dynamic or even ironic ways. Literature, by virtue of its ironic force, undermines "the fantasy of authority."[40]

For the first time, he exposes to the people a voice that, in a sense, undermines its own authority. This kind of speech is not that of a master. His knowledge is not in possession of itself. His testimony to the people calls on them to *hear* him and his unconscious knowledge in a new way: "One does not have to *possess* or *own* the truth, in order to effectively *bear witness* to it."[41]

He surrenders the posture of privileged messenger, speaking in God's name. Now, he speaks without himself exhausting the meaning of his words. Through these final speeches there runs a powerful current, connecting moments. He tells the story of his thwarted prayer—"Let me cross over . . ."; he speaks repeatedly of the fact he is not crossing over, while his audience is crossing over; he says, "God has not given you a heart to know, eyes to see, ears to hear . . ." In sensing the current between such moments, the midrash spins the thread of Moses' unconscious knowledge. The people listen silently, listen with a difference, as unspoken parts of his intimate experience emerge: sacrificial love, anger, disappointment, reproach.

SEEKING HEARTLAND

Why does Moses choose to descend from his pedestal of privileged knowing? Perhaps, simply, in order to *cross over* to his people before he dies. He is now the storyteller, whose authority lies in his approaching death. As the storyteller, he reaches across the gap between teacher and student, analyst and patient. His real life is concentrated in the unforgettable force of his final narratives:

> . . . not only a man's knowledge or wisdom, but, above all, his real life—and this is the stuff that stories are made of—first assumes transmissible form at the moment of his death. Just as a sequence of images is set in motion inside a man as his life comes to an end—unfolding the views of himself under which he has encountered himself without being aware of it—suddenly in his expressions and looks the unforgettable emerges and imparts to everything concerning him that authority which even the poorest wretch in dying possesses for the living around him. This authority is at the very source of the story.[42]

But Moses is also, even before the explicit poetry of chapters 32–33, the poet. In his last speeches, he positions himself, as a poet, at the edge of his own being. His words are in passage, reaching through time. Paul Celan describes the lonely flight of the poem:

> A poem . . . can be a message in a bottle, sent out in the—not always greatly hopeful—belief that somewhere and some-time it could wash up on land, on heartland perhaps.[43]
>
> The poem is lonely. It is lonely and en route. Its author stays with it.[44]

Here is the paradox: the poem is essentially dialogue, but it is lonely, not greatly hopeful, yet still hopeful of a hearing. "Hear o Israel . . . !" As poet-storyteller, Moses yields his authority and unappeasably seeks out "heartland" for his poem: "I on the way to myself."[45] He invites his people to a new kind of listening, and seeing, and knowing.

This means acknowledging that he, too, is in ignorance of his own full meaning—the condition that Felman calls, "the poetic ignorance of his own knowledge."[46] His original response to God's call (*Moshe! Moshe!* [Ex. 3:4]) had been, *Hineni—Here I am!* For Levinas, this translates as *"me voici!"* Paul Ricoeur in turn translates this as "It's me here"—"Who am I, so incon-stant, that *nevertheless* you can count on me?"[47] For Ricoeur, this expresses a "trust in the power to say, in the power to do, in the power to *recognize oneself as a character in a narrative."*

In the ethical moment of encounter with the Other, Moses responded out of the anguish of his fragmented identity that, *nevertheless,* trusts that he is indeed a character in a narrative. His complex response is the "chord" effect of *Hineni* and *Mi anochi?—*"It's me here!" and "Who am I?"

It is this trust that, in his last months, he transfers; he *goes across* from his relation with God to his relation with the people. At the end of a life of conveying God's words to them and of speaking on their behalf to God, he now addresses them as a storyteller, as a poet.

He presents himself to them—*Hineni*—without omniscience

or omnipotence, but with the trust that he is indeed a character in the narrative. Perhaps this is why the Torah calls him "the most humble man (*anav*) on the face of the earth" (Num. 12:3). Perhaps Moses' *anava* is precisely this deep knowledge of being haunted by history as well as mysteriously attuned to the call of the Other.

BEARING THE WEIGHT

Levinas writes of the *weight* of the other's suffering that threatens to overwhelm one:

> The language of the Old Testament is so suspicious of any rhetoric which never stammers that it has as its chief prophet a man "slow of speech and of tongue." . . . This kerygma . . . does not forget the *weight of the world*, the inertia of men, the dullness of their understanding.[48]

Perhaps Moses' resistance to assuming this burden of the world is a defense against the people's pain, which is also his. To *bear* them like an unborn or just-born child would be to expose himself to their utter helplessness, which is also his. He is solicited by their pain, which is also his. Their appeals and demands drain away his strength "like a woman," as the midrash puts it on several occasions.[49]

But in the end, he acknowledges that he is implicated in their inertia, even in their dullness. A certain gentleness ("douceur") forms in him because of this people, as he turns himself to his maternal role. Bearing their weight becomes in his imagination living out this maternal relation with the inconceivable "gentleness" (*douceur*) of which Levinas speaks. At first, the confusion of masculine and feminine roles seems to Moses grotesque; but in the end, when he tells the people of his rejected prayer, complex unconscious resonances, amplified in the midrash, become audible in his voice.

At first, on the heights of Sinai, God had to tell him, *Lech red*—"Go on down" (Ex. 19:24; 32:7) to the people; God had to eject him repeatedly, "for the sake of Israel," from his encounter with the divine. In the end, God harshly rejects his prayer and sends him down, with the force of his whole desire-life, to a new encounter with his people. The ongoing tension between intimacy with God and intimacy with his people modulates to a new key in these last speeches.

"I AM BORN"

If Deuteronomy is Moses' autobiographical moment, then it clearly has many lacunae. Among the many things that Moses does not tell his people are the stories of his birth and of his death. He gives no account of his nursing experience, of his helpless and handled condition as he was passed between mothers and worlds. To have included an account of his birth in his autobiography would have put him in the false position of the adult who recounts what he has heard from others, with the authority of his own adult *I*.

A famous example of this kind of birth autobiography is the opening chapter of *David Copperfield*. The narrator describes the details of his life preceding and including his own birth. Increasingly, he inserts himself as the knowing narrator, ignoring the fact that all these early stories come to him from others. A certain "denial of infancy"[50] seeps into his ever more authoritative account of his infant history. This opening chapter is titled "I Am Born." To tell the story of his infant *I*, his speechless, unformed self, by mobilizing all the resources of his adult self is his impossible, yet necessary, narrative task.

In Moses' autobiographical account of himself to his people, he does not speak of his early life before the wilderness. He has no chapter titled "I Am Born." But his final speeches do, in a sense, present him as being as speechless and helpless as an infant. He has reached the end of his effective life. Little remains within his power at this stage. But this gives him a different kind of power.

He could not answer God, so he now turns to the people with his many words. The unspoken weight of their shared history haunts his story of God's rejection. Implicitly, he reproaches them for failing to give him a hearing; and thus gains, perhaps, a hearing at last. He is both active and acted on: embodied, prostrating himself before them, susceptible, ironical, and powerful all at once.

WRITING IN TEARS

As for his death, he refers to it only in the context of a melancholy comment on the people's rebelliousness (Deut. 31:27). He has, it seems, the darkest expectations of their future "after my death." The meaning of his death, then, is limited, in his account, to its presumed effect on their future history. But, for obvious reasons, he cannot include the experience of his own death in his final narrative.

However, the narrative of "his own book," as it is finally written "by the hand of Moses," does narrate his death. Before he dies, he writes "his own book"—which includes an account of his dying. The impossible but necessary project of writing his own death—the last eight verses, particularly—becomes the subject of evocative rabbinic discussion.

On the one hand, how can he record his own death? Who, then, wrote the words "Moses died there" (Deut. 34:5)? R. Yehuda declares, "Up to that point, Moses wrote the text; from that point, Joshua wrote the last eight verses of the Torah." On the other hand, as R. Shimeon protests, "Can we imagine the scroll of the Torah being short of one word? . . . No, we must say that up to that point, God dictated and Moses repeated the words and wrote; and from that point, God dictated and Moses wrote *in tears*."[51]

The paradox is striking: the idea that the last eight verses were written by Joshua provides a rational solution, but compromises the integrity of Moses' prophecy (the Five Books of Moses). R. Shimeon's view is that Moses writes of his own death—but without repeating the words and with tears in his eyes.

Moses' way of writing the last eight verses, according to R. Shimeon, is different from the writing process of the rest of the Torah. The image of Moses, writing in tears, conveys the impression of a Moses who acknowledges his own susceptibility, his sadness, and the complexity of his embodied condition. Even as he writes in the apparent self-sufficiency of the past tense and the third person—"*Moses died there . . .*"—his lips cannot frame the words; his body sheds tears.

These last words are, and are not, his. The apparent sovereignty of his narrative is accompanied by the emotion of its protagonist. The perspective is almost that of the subject who is writing of himself as though he were another. Like the death of another, his death affects him. Like the people who weep for him, he mourns for himself.

"Death—as the death of the other— . . . is emotion *par excellence*, affection or being affected *par excellence*."[52] In every death, Levinas writes, is shown the nearness of the neighbor, and the responsibility of the survivor. The apparent self-possession expressed in "he wrote in tears" breaks down into a complex image of Moses as his own dying neighbor.

A startling reading of this Talmudic description appears in several commentaries: Moses wrote the last words *with tears—* in place of ink.[53] He writes of his own death in invisible ink, which becomes legible only after his death. Suddenly, we see Moses as both writing and not writing his death. He acts, and simultaneously he is affected by his human finitude. He completes his own book, but his mastery is tempered by his sense of *lacrimae rerum*, "the tears of things." His tears are the very medium of the record, which becomes legible only after he is gone.

This too is part of his last communication to his people. He plays neither the masterful hero nor the victim drowned in a sea of self-regard and self-pity. His end responds to his beginning, his death to his birth. Both are—impossibly—narrated by him, in his written text of the Five Books of Moses.

We remember how his birth narrative gave us an account of what Pharaoh's daughter saw as she opened the basket: "And she saw him, the child (*ba-yeled*). And behold, the youth (*na'ar*) was crying" (Ex. 2:6). Unlike his birth mother who is moved to hide him for three months when she "saw that he was *good*," (2:2)—beautiful? radiant with divine light?—the princess is moved by the sight of the *crying* baby. There is something precocious, almost uncanny, about the voice of this infant; his cry has a power beyond his years. But, objects R. Nehemia, if you say that, you make him a *ba'al moom*—the bearer of an abnormality.[54]

What the princess sees is not the conventional image of a crying baby. This child is dense with contradictions, beautiful and blemished, helpless and powerful. She instantly recognizes the symbolic tragedy in his anguished wail. She takes pity on him as a human, endangered life—representative of the pain of his people.

At the beginning and the end of his life, Moses is speechless, weeping. He takes divine dictation, without uttering the words, as he once wailed wordlessly under the princess's gaze. His tears affect others; after his death, they are reconstituted into the wholeness of the Torah. Almost literally, he *puts himself* into his writing. Are these tears weakness? Or are they the final gift he leaves to and for his people? How else will they "understand" that they have not yet understood?

A HUMAN LIFE

Kafka writes of Moses:

He is on the track of Canaan all his life; it is incredible that
he should see the land only when on the verge of death. The
dying vision of it can only be intended to illustrate how incomplete a moment is human life, incomplete because a life
like this could last forever and still be nothing but a moment.
Moses fails to enter Canaan not because his life is too short
but because it is a human life.[55]

The humanity of Moses' life is for Kafka a matter of its incompleteness. "Nothing but a moment," his life illustrates the
interrupted nature of human desire. We have suggested that
Moses' desire shifts to fill other contours. In his last months,
Moses reaches out in displaced desire to his people. As never
before, he is implicated with them and their vital requirements.
Between the wailing infant and the dying teacher, a human life
arches.

Personal and transpersonal, his voice becomes in later mystical thought the quintessential voice of Israel, of its scholars,
of the Messiah himself. He becomes the soul-root of Israel, the
very type of its creative students. When someone had a brilliant insight in the House of Study, he would be congratulated:
Moses, you have spoken well![56]

In the words and wordlessness of his life, Moses is haunted
not only by the past—the history of the patriarchs, of the Egyptian holocaust—but, in a real sense, by the future. The future
sends out radiations during his infancy and early years. At the
Burning Bush, revelation and mystery claim him: God names
Himself, "*I shall be Who I shall be.*" A fire that is never consumed
draws him aside toward a future self, a historical role that he
passionately resists. "Who am I?" For seven days, according
to the midrash, he resists God's call, provoking, in the end, His
anger.

Thus a life is set in motion in which, through vision and conflict, Moses plays out the demands of his destiny. His humanity is revealed to him in the wilderness: a personal life that finds expression in the speeches of his final months. The man of God who had always spoken *for* Israel now speaks for his personal self in a way that stirs depths in those who hear him. When he reaches out to his people in the fraught language of relationship, he makes himself unforgettable. Veiled and unveiled, he remains lodged in the Jewish imagination, where, in his uncompleted humanity, he comes to represent the yet-unattained but attainable messianic future.

Introduction

1. Thomas H. Ogden, *Subjects of Analysis* (Northvale, NJ: Jason Aronson Inc., 1994), 1–2.

2. All translations from biblical texts are by the author.

3. See Deut. Rabba 3:12 and 7:11.

4. B. Baba Batra: "Moses wrote the story of Balaam, the book of Job, and his book."

5. See Alexander Nehamas, *The Art of Living* (Berkeley, CA: University of California Press, 1998), 91–92, for a discussion of a similar motif in Plato's account of Socrates.

6. Brachot 32a.

7. Marina Tsvetaeva, *Dark Elderberry Branch: Poems of Marina Tsvetaeva*, trans. Jean Valentine and Ilya Kaminsky (Farmington, ME: Alice James Books, 2012), 32.

8. Strikingly, the Talmud (B. Sanhedrin 21b) reads this as referring to the obligation for each individual to write his own copy of the Torah: "Write *for yourselves* . . ."

9. Osip Mandelstam, *Stolen Air*, trans. Christian Wiman (New York: Ecco, 2012), xl.

Chapter One: Identities

1. Rashi to Ex. 1:8.

2. See Elaine Scarry, *The Body in Pain* (New York: Oxford University Press, 1985), 19–22 and passim.

3. See Mei HaShiloah Shemot (2). He reads Psalms 66: "Blessed be God Who has not removed my prayer and His love from me" as suggesting that the human possibility of prayer is in itself an expression of divine love.

4. Lekach Tov in Torah Shelemah Shemoth 126.

5. Cathy Caruth, *Unclaimed Experience* (Baltimore: The Johns Hopkins University Press, 1996), 17–18.

6. Ibid., 61.

7. Charles Dickens, *Hard Times* (New York: Signet Classics, 1961), 198.

8. See Shemot Rabba 2:7: "God said to Moses, Do you not feel that I am in distress, just as Israel is in distress? Be aware that the place from which I speak to you is in the midst of thorns, I am their partner in distress!"

9. The midrashic proof-texts accompanying such passages of involvement are typically, "I am with him in his distress" (Ps. 91), and "In all their troubles He was troubled" (Isa. 63:9). God is *with* His people, He is *in* their troubles. Like them, He is submerged and seeks to emerge.

10. Shemot Rabba 3:1.

11. Exodus Rabba 1:28.

12. Tzror HaMor.

13. B. Sotah 12b. The Talmud may be reading *et ha-yeled* as "*with* the child."

14. Marina Tsvetaeva, *Dark Elderberry Branch: Poems of Marina Tsvetaeva*, trans. Jean Valentine and Ilya Kaminsky (Farmington, ME: Alice James Books, 2012), 40.

15. T. S. Eliot, "East Coker," in *Four Quartets*, V, 179 (San Diego: Harcourt Inc., 1943).

16. B. Brachot 32a.

17. Martin Buber, *Moses: The Revelation and the Covenant* (New York: Humanity Books, 1958), 59.

18. *Massa*, "burden," is the term used in the prophetic books to refer to the commissioning of the prophet.

19. See Lev. Rabba 1:3, B. Batra 15a, for other names identifying Moses.

20. See Is. 63:11.

21. Shemot Rabba 3:20.

22. See Françoise Davoine and Jean-Max Gaudillière, *History beyond Trauma* (New York: Other Press, 2004), 254. In Rabelais's *Gargantua and Pantagruel*, the hero hears voices at sea which turn out to come from the submerged site of a naval battle in which all disappeared with all their possessions. The terrifying noises of the battle "froze in the air. But now that the hardship of winter has passed . . . they are melting and are heard."

23. Shemot Rabba 3:1.

24. George Eliot, *Daniel Deronda* (New York: Oxford University Press, 1984), 642.

25. W. G. Sebald, *Austerlitz*, trans. Anthea Bell (New York: Random House, 2001).

26. W. G. Sebald, *Campo Santo*, trans. Anthea Bell (New York: The Modern Library), 118.

27. B. Shabbat 101b.

28. See Jorge Luis Borges, "Kafka's Precursors," in *Labyrinths* (New York: New Directions, 1962), 201.

29. Beit Yaakov, Shemot, 74.

30. B. Sotah 12a.

31. See Anne Carson, *Economy of the Unlost* (Princeton: Princeton University Press, 1999), 109. The quotation is from Celan's "Sprich auch du," translated by John Felstiner in his *Paul Celan, Poet, Survivor, Jew* (New Haven: Yale University Press, 1995), 79.

32. Felstiner, *Paul Celan*, 94.

33. Carson, *Economy of the Unlost*, 29.

34. Ibid.

35. Felstiner, *Paul Celan*, xvii.

36. Carson, *Economy of the Unlost*, 30.

37. Felstiner, *Paul Celan*, 172. "Pallaksch. Pallaksch." is Hölderlin's expression for "sometimes yes, sometimes no."

38. Friedrich Nietzsche, *Thus Spoke Zarathustra*, trans. Walter Kaufmann (New York: Viking Press, 1954), 36.

39. Julie Cooper, "Moses the Modest Law-Giver" (unpublished article).

40. Martin Buber, *Moses* (New York: Humanity Books, 1998), 59. Cited in Cooper, 18.

41. See Herbert Marks, "On Prophetic Stammering," in *The Book and the Text*, ed. Regina Schwartz (Cambridge, MA: Basil Blackwell, 1990).

42. Stephen Frosh, *For and Against Psychoanalysis* (London: Routledge, 1997), 183.

43. Mei HaShiloach Tissa 1.

44. B. Brachot 7a.

45. Emmanuel Levinas, "Revelation in the Jewish Tradition," *The Levinas Reader*, ed. Sean Hand (Cambridge, MA: Blackwell, 1989), 197.

46. Maimonides Moses, *The Guide of the Perplexed*. Trans. Shlomo Pines (Chicago: University of Chicago Press, 1963), 7.

47. Maimonides (1963), 123.

48. B. Menachot 29b.

49. Tanchuma Pikudei 9.

50. Cited in Stephen Frosh, *For and Against Psychoanalysis* (London: Routledge, 2006), 181.

51. Cited in Jane Gallop, *Reading Lacan* (Ithaca: Cornell University Press, 1985), 84.

52. In Rashi's version of this midrash (to 38:8), the woman is *me-shadel* her husband: "open," "swing," hence "seduce."

53. See, e.g., Rashi and Ramban to 3:14: God's identity will evolve in the context of evolving human realities. It has a "mirroring" function.

54. Sebald, *Austerlitz*, 27.

55. Ibid., 136.

56. See Scarry, *The Body in Pain*, 19–22.

57. Sefat Emet VaYikra, 72.

58. Michael Herr, *Dispatches*, quoted in Caruth, *Unclaimed Experience*, 10.

59. Caruth, *Unclaimed Experience*, 11.

60. I owe this image to Ben Lerner, *Leaving the Atocha Station* (Minneapolis: Coffee House Press, 2011), 14.

Chapter Two: The Murmuring Deep

1. Moses will voice the *lamah* note repeatedly as he attempts to bridge the gap between God and the people. See, e.g., Ex. 32:11; 32:12; Num. 11:11.

2. The ambiguity is expressed in the doubling of "He spoke. . . . And He said" (6:2)—representing "hard" and "soft" speech.

3. Shemot Rabba 5:27.

4. The more skeptical view is voiced in the midrash by R. Ishmael.

5. Several midrashic sources spell out the horror of Egyptian atrocities: babies falling into the clay and folded into the Egyptian building machine.

6. See Ramban to Genesis 47:28.

7. This section was inspired by an unpublished lecture by Steven Frosh, "Marginalia," presented at the London School of Jewish Studies in July 2007.

8. See the translation of *tehom* in A. M. Silbermann, trans., *Chumash with Rashi's Commentary* (Jerusalem: Silbermann Family, by arrangement with Routledge and Kegan Paul Ltd., 1973). This translation is based on Abraham Benisch, *Jewish School and Family Bible* (London: James Darling, 1851), the first Jewish translation of the Bible into English.

9. See Slavoj Žižek, *The Parallax View* (Cambridge, MA: MIT Press, 2009), 154.

10. Alphonso Lingis, *The Community of Those Who Have Nothing in Common* (Bloomington: Indiana University Press, 1994), 122.

11. See note 7 of this chapter.

12. In the Zohar, Moses is credited with being "voice without speech."

13. Lingis, *Community of Those Who Have Nothing in Common*, 69.

14. Ibid., 75.

15. Ibid., 91.

16. Quoted in Adam Phillips, *Terror and Experts* (Cambridge, MA: Harvard University Press, 1965), 13.

17. André Neher, *The Exile of the Word* (Philadelphia: Jewish Publication Society of America, 1981), 68.

18. Mei HaShiloach 1, VaEra.

19. In the Zohar, the "soft" tone of *Emor* is commonly identified as a whisper.

20. Mei HaShiloach 1, Emor.

21. Lingis, *Community of Those Who Have Nothing in Common*, 73.

22. My thanks again to Stephen Frosh for his reference to Agamben.

23. Giorgio Agamben, *Remnants of Auschwitz* (New York: Zone Books, 1999), 33–34.

24. Ibid., 37.

25. Ibid.

26. Ibid., 38.

27. Ibid., 39.

28. Ibid., 120–21.

29. Ibid., 150.

30. Slavoj Žižek, *The Abyss of Freedom / Ages of the World*, 50. Cited in Eric Santner, *On the Psychotheology of Everyday Life* (Chicago: University of Chicago Press, 2001), 6–7.

31. Santner, *On the Psychotheology of Everyday Life*, 7. He terms this "out-of-jointness," *Egyptomania*: "The enigmas of the ancient Egyptians were also enigmas for the Egyptians themselves."

32. Maharal, *Gevurot Hashem*, ch. 28.

33. Maharal cites another Talmudic passage (Ta'anit 11b) that describes Moses as serving in the Tabernacle during the eight days of its inauguration, clothed in a pure white garment, "without an

imra" (a fringe, or cuff—also, speech). Moses' outward appearance reflects the immaculate purity of his being, uncompromised by language, by the fray-able edge of things, which requires reinforcement. In this, Moses' garment is unlike that of the priests who will take over from him in the Tabernacle after the period of inauguration.

34. See Rashi to 7:15.

35. Rashi to 7:15.

36. See Erich Neumann, *The Origins and History of Consciousness*, Bollingen Series (Princeton: Princeton University Press, 1970), ch. 1.

37. Samuel Beckett, *Krapp's Last Tape*, quoted in Gabriel Josipovici, *On Trust* (New Haven: Yale University Press, 1999), 237.

38. Stanley Cavell, *The Senses of Walden* (Chicago: University of Chicago Press, 1972), 33–34.

39. Christopher Bollas, *The Shadow of the Object* (London: Free Association Books, 1987), 277–83.

40. In general, the word is used as a collective reference to the poor, the oppressed, the social outcast. For an illuminating study of this concept in rabbinic thought, see Shmuel Lewis, *And Before Honor—Humility* (in Hebrew)—particularly ch. 5.

41. Victor Turner, *Dramas, Fields, and Metaphors* (Ithaca: Cornell University Press, 1974), 234.

42. Ibid., 268.

43. Ibid., 274.

44. The midrash speaks of *anvatanut*, a variation of *anava*.

45. B. Megilla 31a.

46. Shmuel Lewis, *And before Honor—Humility* (Jerusalem: Magnes Press, 2013), 149 ff. (in Hebrew).

47. Mechilta d'Rabbi Yishmael, 14, 50. Cited in Lewis, *And before Honor—Humility*, 148.

48. The history of Kaspar Hauser, the child without language who is suddenly thrust into the social world, is the extreme example of the fascination that we feel for the bare humanity represented by such figures. Thousands of articles have been written about Kaspar. Beyond the technical interest in the process of late

acquisition of language, there are the philosophical conundrums aroused by this history. Something purely human, daunting in its purity, confronts the structured society. Kaspar met with extraordinary tenderness, curiosity, awe, horror, as well as murderous hatred. He is, in some way, in all his difference, ourselves. See Werner Herzog's film *The Enigma of Kaspar Hauser* (1974). Herzog focuses on this quality of purity, which is the motif of most of his films.

Chapter Three: Moses Veiled and Unveiled

1. B. Brachot 32a.

2. Gaston Bachelard, *The Poetics of Space* (Boston: Beacon Press, 1964), 222.

3. Ibid., 223.

4. Ibid., 224.

5. Rashi's source is Tanchuma Tissa.

6. B. Brachot 7a.

7. Beit Yaakov Tissa, 68.

8. In the original midrash (Tanchuma Tissa, 37), various alternative images play round the theme of the rays of light. Sparks of the divine inhabit Moses' face. Or, the middle section of the Tablets, held by neither God nor Moses, becomes the transitional space from which the rays emerge. Or, the left-over ink in Moses' pen, as he writes the Torah, is wiped over his head, producing light. Each image, in its own fragmentary way, conveys something of a present absence.

9. Ralph Waldo Emerson, "Self-Reliance," in *Selected Essays* (New York: Penguin Books, 1982), 176.

10. Stanley Cavell, *Conditions Handsome and Unhandsome* (Chicago: University of Chicago Press, 1990), 57.

11. See Deuteronomy 5:5.

12. Jacques Lacan and Slavoj Žižek develop a theme from horror movies: the *undead*, representing the failure to symbolize, haunt human beings with a sinister vitality, like zombies.

13. Rashi to 32:1, citing B. Shabbat 89.

14. D. W. Winnicott, *Playing and Reality* (London: Routledge, 1982), 97.

15. B. Shabbat 88b.

16. See Rashi to 32:9: "They turn the bony back of their necks towards those who rebuke them, refusing to listen."

17. *Difficult Freedom* is the title of Emmanuel Levinas's collection of essays on Jewish themes.

18. Rieff, *Freud: The Mind of the Moralist* (Chicago: University of Chicago Press, 1979), 166.

19. Translated from Immanuel Kant, *Idee zu einer allgemeinen Geschichte in weltbürgerlicher Absicht*, 6. Satz, Spiegel Online Kultur/ Project Gutenberg–DE, http://gutenberg.spiegel.de/buch/-3506/1.

20. B. Brachot 32a.

21. See B. Baba Batra 109b; Judges 18:30. The young house priest is named Yonatan son of Gershom son of Me*n*asheh. Since Menasheh is written with the letter *nun* suspended in the text, the Rabbis read it as referring to *M-sh-eh*, Moses.

22. Rashi to Ex. 32:10.

23. Yochanan Muffs describes this prophetic paradox as similar to the role of Her Majesty's Loyal Opposition in the British parliament. See *Love and Joy* (New York: Jewish Theological Seminary of America, 1992), ch. 1.

24. B. Brachot 32a.

25. Bachelard, *The Poetics of Space*, 220.

26. Cf. B. Shabbat 89a.

27. Zohar 67b.

28. See the commentary of Seforno to Ex. 32:19, quoting Jeremiah's lament: "You exult while performing your evil deeds!" (Jer. 11:15).

29. See Seforno to 32:21.

30. B. Shabbat 87b.

31. Sifrei Bamidbar 84 and Sifrei Zuta to Numbers 10:35.

32. See Sifrei Zuta Bamidbar, 10:35, which cites Isaiah 63:9 ("In all their suffering I suffer too") and Psalm 91:15 ("If he calls Me I shall answer; I am with him in suffering") as classic proof-texts.

33. The version in Sotah 12, as quoted by Rashi to 24:10, reads the end of the vision—"like the essence of the heaven for purity"

—"When they were redeemed there was light and joy in His presence."

34. This is the literal wording in Ex. 24:10.

35. A powerful midrashic narrative suggests that Hur, Aaron's son, is killed in the mob-ecstasy—a murder that is repressed in the text (Rashi to Ex. 32:5). Hur is understood to represent Aaron, who then tries to assuage their frenzy. Aaron, in turn, is a displacement for Moses, who is the target of the people's unconscious hatred. See Or HaChaim to Ex. 32:1.

36. Exodus Rabba 46:1.

37. B. Brachot 32a.

38. Emerson, "Self-Reliance," 176.

39. Virginia Woolf, *Diary*, vol. 2 (New York: Harcourt Brace, 1980).

40. Stanley Cavell, *Pursuits of Happiness* (Cambridge, MA: Harvard University Press, 1981), 37.

41. J. Hillis Miller, *Illustration* (Cambridge, MA: Harvard University Press, 1992), 145.

42. Ibid., 135.

43. Ibid., 134.

Chapter Four: Moses in the Family

1. *Vayigdal*—"And he grew up"—is used twice, once when he is weaned and handed back to Pharaoh's daughter, and again when he emerges from the palace. It seems to signify a new stage of development.

2. Rashi to 4:10.

3. Robert M. Cover, "Nomos and Narrative," *Harvard Law Review* (November 1983), 22.

4. Regarding Aaron's role as prophet and leader, see, e.g., Ezekiel 20. This passage is used as a proof-text in several midrashic texts.

5. Tanchuma Shemot, 27.

6. This is the impact of God's anger on Moses' life: his brother, who was a simple Levite, now becomes High Priest, while Moses is demoted to simple Levite. See B. Zevachim 102a.

7. Julia Kristeva, *Black Sun* (New York: Columbia University Press, 1989), 43.

8. Ibid., 53.

9. Exodus Rabba 37:4.

10. The midrashic term *invetanut* derives from *anav*, humble, which the Torah, in a rare moment of explicit portrayal, describes as Moses' dominant characteristic: "Moses was a very humble man, more so than any man on earth" (Num. 12:3). The midrashic narrative focuses on a specific moment when Moses demonstrates his greatness in an act of humility in relation to his brother Aaron.

11. Exodus Rabba 2:13.

12. See Sefat Emet Likkutim, Exodus, Tetzaveh.

13. See Rashi to Ex. 6:1.

14. A similar tension of presence and absence is found in the liturgical timing of the Torah portion, which is usually read in the week when 7 Adar occurs—the date of Moses' birth and death. A mythic birth-death theme haunts Moses' life.

15. Keats, *Letters* (London: Oxford University Press, 1954), 53.

16. Ibid., 50.

17. See Ha'amek Davar, Sefat Emet, Pri Tzaddik. Moses, the *non-speaker*, is both the passive medium registering God's Torah and, in these commentaries, the creator of *Torat Moshe*—Moses' Torah—the product of intellectual labor and creativity. Mystical traditions lie behind these retellings of Moses' story.

18. Ha'amek Davar cites R. Tarfon, who used to celebrate a brilliant interpretation with the words *kaftor va-ferach!*—"A knob and a blossom!" (Genesis Rabba 91:12).

19. Tanchuma Shemini, 3.

20. In this "chameleon" mode, Moses reminds us of John Keats's description of the "poetical Character . . . which has no self—it is everything and nothing. . . . When I am in a room with People . . . then not myself goes home to myself: but the identity of every one in the room begins so to press upon me that I am in a very little time annihilated—not only among Men; it would be the same in a Nursery of children . . ." (Keats, *Letters*, 172).

21. Rashi engages in elaborate wordplay to make the identifi-

cation of the Cushite woman. The general gist is that Tzippora is beautiful, inside and out, so that the only reason for Moses' abstinence is the consuming nature of his prophecy.

22. Exodus Rabba 1:17.

23. *Gezera*—"decree"—derives from the root *g-z-r*, which means "cutting." The decree implies incisive separation, exclusion of the forbidden.

24. Exodus Rabba 1:25.

25. B. Sotah 9b.

26. "He is our brother, our flesh," Judah says of Joseph (Gen. 37:27).

27. J. L. Austin, *How to Do Things with Words* (New York: Oxford University Press, 1970).

28. B. Sotah 17a.

29. Midrash Bamidbar Rabba 18:8.

30. Psalm 115:17. See also, among many other examples, Psalms 94:17; 88:12.

31. The biblical word *vayichar*, without the word *af*, is often translated in this way in the midrash, as though it referred to a generalized emotional agitation.

32. See Sefat Emet Shemot, p. 84 (*U-bil'shon ha-passuk . . . kabbalat bnei yisrael*).

33. The Hebrew word for "two lips"—*sefatayim*—is also the word for "two edges."

34. The idiom, *le-hanik le . . .* (nursing for . . .) is used in Miriam's proposal and in the princess's speech to Moses' mother. Interestingly, when she nurses him, the text drops the *le-* idiom—simply, "she nursed him."

35. B. Sanhedrin 110a. See also Rashi to 16:12.

36. Rashbam reads this as refusing to submit to judgment.

37. See Or HaChayim to 16:12.

38. Jacques Lacan, Seminar XXI, November 1974.

39. See Rashi's translation of "uncircumcised" as "blocked," on Exodus 6:12.

40. *Machloket* (dissension, schismatic behavior) is seen in midrashic sources as Korach's fatal flaw.

41. G. K. Chesterton, *Orthodoxy* (New York: Doubleday, 1959), 19–20.

42. Walter Benjamin, *Understanding Brecht*, trans. Anna Bostock (London: Verso, 1983), 73.

43. Mei HaShiloah, 2, *Korach (K'tiv . . .).*

44. See Marion Milner, *The Suppressed Madness of Sane Men* (London: Routledge, 1988), 208.

45. Emmanuel Levinas, *Totality and Infinity* (Pittsburgh: Duquesne University Press, 1969), 207.

46. Ibid., 171.

47. Levinas, "Revelation in the Jewish Tradition," in *The Levinas Reader*, ed. Sean Hand (Oxford: Blackwell, 1989), 209.

48. *The Levinas Reader*, 197.

49. Leonard Cohen writes of this moment: "Ring the bells that still can ring / Forget your perfect offering / There is a crack, a crack in everything / That's how the light gets in" ("Anthem").

50. See Pirkei Avot 5:8.

51. B. Sanhedrin 108a.

52. Typically, the biblical verse is composed of two halves, separated by a punctuation mark, the *etnachta*. This verse ends in "mid-verse."

53. B. Sanhedrin 110a.

54. Sefat Emet, Vayikra (Pesach), 79.

Chapter Five: "Moses wrote his own book"

1. B. Baba Batra 14b.

2. In line with this reading, Moses fails to find *navonim*, perceptive, intuitive people; he finds only "wise and distinguished men" (Deut. 1:13, 15).

3. Cf. Ex. 4:1.

4. Rashbam and Ibn Ezra (short version), Hizkuni. One assumption of this view is that the Hebrews too spoke Egyptian.

5. Ibn Ezra (long version).

6. Even Egyptian babies are to be killed, because of an astrological prediction that the Israelite savior—whether Hebrew or Egyptian—is to be born on that day. See Rashi to Ex. 1:22.

7. Torah Shelema 2:[51].

8. Rashi to 2:6.

9. B. Sotah 12b.

10. See chap. 1.

11. Rashi to 20:12.

12. Yalkut Shimoni 763.

13. Ralph Waldo Emerson, "The Poet," in *Selected Essays* (New York: Penguin Books, 1982), 279, 265.

14. Rashi to 17:12. See also Ramban to 17:9.

15. B. Shabbat 87b.

16. B. Eruvin 54a.

17. In rabbinic thought, this is a constitutive description of humanity, like eating and drinking.

18. John Berger, *The Sense of Sight* (New York: Vintage International, 1985), 194–96.

19. The imagery of *l'hotzi*—bringing forth—persists throughout the biblical depiction of Moses. At the Burning Bush, he "brings forth" his hand from his bosom, once to find it leprous, and again to find it healed.

20. Exodus Rabba 43:1.

21. It is striking that *ma'amid panim* suggest the idea of "putting up a front, putting the best face on it"—in modern Hebrew, pretending.

22. T. S. Eliot, "The Love Song of J. Alfred Prufrock."

23. Yohanan Muffs, "His Majesty's Loyal Opposition: A Study in Prophetic Intercession," *Conservative Judaism* 33:3 (1978–1980): 25–37.

24. B. Shabbat 89a. Another Talmudic narrative of this kind tells of the High Priest ascending to the higher worlds to find God praying *before His own face* for His compassionate aspect to overwhelm His anger. God then bids the High Priest, "Ishmael My son, bless Me!" The High Priest blesses God with the very words of His own prayer to Himself. And God "nods His head" in acknowledgment (B. Brachot 7a).

25. Song of Songs Rabba 1:44.

26. Ruth Rabba 7:2.

27. See Ex. 25:8 for the classic proof-text.

28. Emmanuel Levinas, *Totality and Infinity* (Pittsburgh: Duquesne University Press, 1969), 150.

29. See Rashi to Num. 11:15; B. Brachot 32a on Num. 14:16; Rashi on Deut. 5:24. Sometimes, Moses feels "as weak as a woman" in the face of the people's intransigence; other times, he protests at God's presumed helplessness in the eyes of the nations.

30. Often, his present account differs significantly from the "real time" account, particularly in the words that he remembers speaking. The reshapings of memory are everywhere in these last speeches. His earlier references to himself and his speech problems were largely couched in the negative, delineating an absence —"heavy of mouth," "not a man of words"—or a *too-muchness*—of uncircumcised lips—and implying unspeakable experience.

31. B. Avoda Zara 5b.

32. See Rashi to 29:6.

33. "Till this day": The question is whether "till" includes "this day" or not. Rashi reads optimistically, citing a midrashic story to indicate that the people have changed.

34. Deuteronomy Rabba 3:12.

35. Deuteronomy Rabba 7:11.

36. Tanchuma Devarim, 1.

37. Bamidbar Rabba 21:15.

38. See, e.g., Exodus 5:1; 5:23; 6:2–8.

39. See Roland Barthes, "Writers, Intellectuals, Teachers," in *Image/Music/Text* (New York: Hill and Wang, 1978), 194–96.

40. *The Claims of Literature: A Shoshana Felman Reader* (New York: Fordham University Press, 2007), 215–16.

41. Shoshana Felman, *Testimony* (New York: Routledge, 1992), 15.

42. Walter Benjamin, "The Storyteller," in *Illuminations* (London: Collins/Fontana Books, 1973), 94.

43. John Felstiner, *Paul Celan* (New Haven: Yale University Press, 1995), 115.

44. Anne Carson, *Economy of the Unlost* (Princeton: Princeton University Press, 1999), 69.

45. Ibid.

46. Shoshana Felman, *Jacques Lacan and the Adventure of Insight* (Cambridge, MA: Harvard University Press, 1987), 94.

47. Donna Orange, *The Suffering Stranger* (New York: Routledge, 2011), 50–51.

48. *The Levinas Reader*, ed. Sean Hand (Oxford: Blackwell, 1989), 197.

49. See, e.g., Rashi to Num. 11:15.

50. See Judith Butler, *Senses of the Subject* (New York: Fordham University Press, 2015), 3.

51. B. Baba Batra 14b–15a. See also B. Menachot 30a.

52. Emmanuel Levinas, *God, Death, and Time*, trans. Bettina Bergo (Stanford: Stanford University Press, 2000), 9.

53. See commentaries of *Ritva*, *Maharsha*, and *Iyyun Yaacov* to B. Baba Batra 15a.

54. B. Sotah 12.

55. Franz Kafka, *Diaries 1914–23*, trans. Martin Greenberg and Hannah Arendt (New York: Schocken Books, 1965), 195–96.

56. B. Shabbat 101b. Cf. Likkutei Moharan 4:5: "Every scholar is associated with Moses . . ."

GENERAL INDEX

SCRIPTURAL INDEX

Rabbinic Works

Jewish Lives is a major series of interpretive
biography designed to illuminate the imprint of Jewish
figures upon literature, religion, philosophy, politics, cultural and
economic life, and the arts and sciences. Subjects are paired with
authors to elicit lively, deeply informed books that explore the
range and depth of Jewish experience from
antiquity through the present.

Jewish Lives is a partnership of Yale University Press
and the Leon D. Black Foundation.

Ileene Smith is editorial director. Anita Shapira
and Steven J. Zipperstein are series editors.